XI'AN

© 2000, 1993 Odyssey Publications Ltd
Maps © 2000, 1993 Odyssey Publications Ltd

Odyssey Publications Ltd, 1003 Kowloon Centre, 29–43 Ashley Road,
Tsim Sha Tsui, Kowloon, Hong Kong
Tel. (852) 2856 3896; Fax. (852) 2565 8004; E-mail: odyssey@asiaonline.net
World Wide Web: www.odysseypublications.com

Distribution in the United Kingdom, Ireland and Europe by
Hi Marketing Ltd, 38 Carver Road, London SE24 9LT, UK

Distribution in the United States of America by
W.W. Norton & Company, Inc., New York

ISBN: 962-217-621-6

Grateful acknowledgement is made to the authors and publishers for permissions granted:
Faber and Faber Limited for *Journey to a War* by W H Auden and Christopher Isherwood © revised edition 1991 W H Auden and Christopher Isherwood; Foreign Languages Press, Beijing for *Tu Fu: Selected Poems* compiled by Feng Chih and translated by Rewi Alley; Kodansha International Ltd for *Lou-lan and Other Stories* by Yasushi Inoue translated by Edward Seidensticker © 1979 Kodansha International Ltd; Hodder and Stoughton for *Alone on the Great Wall* by William Lindesay © Hodder & Stoughton; Thames and Hudson Ltd, London for *China Diary* by Stephen Spender and David Hockney © 1982 Stephen Spender and David Hockney; William Heinemann Limited for *Behind the Wall* by Colin Thubron © 1987 Colin Thubron; Century Publishing Co, London for *China's Sorrow* by Lynn Pan © 1985 Lynn Pan

Managing Editor: Frank Murdoch
Editing and Design: Kevin Bishop
Maps: Au Yeung Chui Kwai, Kevin Bishop
Index: Françoise Parkin

Front cover photograph by Luo Zhong Min; back cover by Kevin Bishop
Photography courtesy of Kevin Bishop 97, 100, 116, 144; China Guide Series 32, 33; Simon Holledge 80; Hong Kong China Photo Tourism Library 10–11, 93; William Lindesay 36; Luo Guoshi and Luo Liangbi 17; Luo Zhong Min 2–3, 41, 45, 52, 84–85, 88, 121; Yang Ling Mausoleum Archaeological Team 64–65, 68, 69, 72, 73; Yu Shi Jun 108–109; Xia Ju Xian 49, 53, 56; Zhang Xue De 40

Production by Twin Age Limited, Hong Kong
Manufactured in China

(*previous pages*) *Just some of the 6,000 terracotta warriors thought to be buried in Pit Number One of the Museum of Terracotta Warriors and Horses of Emperor Qin Shihuangdi, over a third of which have been so far excavated.*

XI'AN

by
Simon Holledge

Revised by
Kevin Bishop

ACKNOWLEDGEMENT
I would like to thank Mr Zhao Li-cheng, Deputy Manager, English Department of
Xi'an CITS and his very able guides, namely Mr Fan Sheng Guang, Mr Zhang Yang
and Ms Lu Yi, for their valuable assistance in updating this guidebook.

CONTENTS

(previous pages) The Big Goose Pagoda (Dayan Ta), first constructed in 652 at the request of the Tang monk Xuanzong following his pilgrimage to India.

LITERARY EXCERPTS

SPECIAL TOPICS

MAPS

(following pages) Loess landscape of the Yellow Earth Plateau, northern Shaanxi Province

An Introduction to Xi'an

The city of Chang'an, site of modern day Xi'an, was the capital of China for longer than any other—a total of some 1,100 years.

The magnificent archaeological and art discoveries in and around the city tell the tale of China's development from prehistoric times until the height of the imperial period. There have been so many astounding finds in the area that it is possible to put only a small proportion on view to the public. Furthermore, so many tombs and sites remain unexcavated that archaeologists seem literally only to have scratched the surface.

Xi'an was at different times the capital of the Zhou, Han, Sui and Tang dynasties. Lying on the Wei River in Shaanxi Province, it commanded the approaches to central China from the mountains of the northwest. It was also the eastern terminus of the old Silk Road along which culture and merchandise was exchanged with peoples as far west as the Mediterranean.

Dubbed 'the land of kings and emperors' by Du Fu, China's most famous poet, Xi'an can trace its origins to the 11th century BC, when the rulers of the Zhou dynasty set up Fenghao, a twin city made up of Fengjing and Haojing, about 16 kilometres (ten miles) southwest of the present site. The city was grid-shaped—a pattern which later became common in Chinese cities. It was said that nine carts could ride abreast on each of the 18 main roads of the grid.

The modern city is plain and business-like, but the narrow residential alleys and street markets bear the flavour of old China. Unlike Beijing, Xi'an's old Ming-dynasty city wall has thankfully been preserved or renovated and testifies to the city's strategic importance down the ages. Whilst development has taken place within the walls the height of the buildings has been contained, and instead the taller buildings and wider boulevards have been constructed outside the old city area.

Easily accessible from Xi'an is Yan'an, where the late Chairman Mao Zedong's followers in the Communist Party built up their strength for the final confrontation with Generalissimo Chiang Kai-shek's Nationalist forces. Chiang was actually captured in his nightgown trying to escape from the hot springs resort near Xi'an by a younger commander, who wanted him to unite with the Communists and fight the Japanese—the famous Xi'an Incident of 1936.

In the eighth century BC, the Zhou dynasty moved its capital from the Wei River valley, downstream to Luoyang on the Yellow River. A ruler of the Kingdom of Qin, in northwest China, established his capital at Xianyang, just northwest of present-day Xi'an. In 221 BC the King of Qin conquered the other feudal kingdoms to become the First Emperor. Qin Shihuangdi, as he became know, imposed an early form of totalitarianism on China. He consolidated and extended the various sections of the Great Wall which was to keep out fierce northern tribesmen. He standardized the Chinese written language, coinage, weights and measures and even the span of cart axles. But his oppressive rule broke down when his son succeeded to the throne, and after a bloody civil war a rebel commander called Liu Bang established the Han dynasty with its capital at the city which was now called Chang'an.

The Han dynasty was a period of great cultural flowering and imperial expansion. Pottery, bronze and iron work, lacquer, precious metal, wall-painting and sculpture of a very high artistic standard survive in impressive quantities. Chang'an was three times the size of Rome at the time.

Qin Shihuangdi died in 210 BC. In accordance with the custom of the time, it is believed, he had his ministers, family members, slaves and horses buried with him—but whether all of them were actually killed, as would have been normal a few centuries earlier, or whether some were buried later as they died naturally, is not clear. The main part of the emperor's tomb is yet to be excavated.

But pottery figures of soldiers and horses leave no doubt that the emperor wanted a bodyguard in the afterlife. There are estimated to be some 8,000 clay warriors, whose existence was discovered by some peasants digging a well in 1974. The pottery figures are slightly larger than life-size and each is different from the others. They wear a variety of uniforms and body-armour, though all have a flowing, knee-length robe and breeches. They wear their hair in elaborate topknots and sport neat moustaches. Some are kneeling in postures which suggest that they once held drawn bows of wood, now decayed. The figures are a fascinating link with the past over a period of 22 centuries. The whole tomb area covers nearly 57 square kilometres (22 square miles).

In AD 25 the Eastern Han dynasty removed the capital to Luoyang. From the third century there ensued a period of civil war and division of China into separate kingdoms, sometimes with rival claimants to the title of emperor. But in 582 the founder of the Sui dynasty, Yang Qian, restored the city as the capital. It was enlarged and improved and a famous Chinese poet wrote of it: 'Ten thousand houses look like a laid-out chessboard.' Merchants and tribute bearers from central and western Asia arrived with exotic products. But the new capital shortly fell to Li Yuan, who established the Tang dynasty. The most famous imperial concubine in Chinese history, the beauty Yang Guifei, and the most famous powerful empress, Wu Zetian, inhabited the imperial palace in the Tang dynasty. In its cultural achievements, the Tang outdid even the Han dynasty, especially in poetry, painting, music, ceramics and calligraphy.

With the fall of the Tang dynasty in AD 907, the capital was removed—after a period of civil war—to the city of Kaifeng in Henan Province in AD 960, and later, when the Jin Tartars invaded north China, to Hangzhou in the east. The Mongols led by Kublai Khan later conquered northern China and in 1271 established their capital at Beijing. The Ming dynasty (1368–1644), while governing from Beijing, rebuilt the inner section of the city and in 1368 renamed it Xi'an, but it was never to be the capital again. The name Xi'an, meaning Western Peace, is represented by two characters in Chinese and hence is correctly spelt with an apostrophe in pinyin. This is to distinguish it from several other single characters that are spelt xian in pinyin, but pronounced differently.

For many years the main tourist attractions of Xi'an have been the Ming-dynasty Drum and Bell towers and the Great Mosque near the city centre, the National Museum of Shaanxi History, Beilin Museum, the Big Goose and Little Goose pagodas, the old city wall, the stone-age site at Banpo, Famen Temple, and above all the terracotta warriors at Lintong, buried in the ground to guard Qin Shihuangdi's tomb. But at the end of September 1999, a new sight was added to the list—Yang Ling, the tomb of Jingdi, the fourth Han emperor, being excavated beside the airport highway. A museum has been opened to display some of the thousands of pottery figurines and animals unearthed there (see page 69 for more information on this site).

There are numerous other imperial tombs that are known to exist together with a large number of satellite tombs, but they have yet to be touched by archaeologists. Though some may have been despoiled by tomb-robbers, others must surely contain remarkable treasures and will take decades to excavate when finally work gets underway.

Although the city is quite heavily industrialized, the Chinese Government has decided to give priority to excavation and restoration of ancient sites and buildings. Unfortunately much damage had already been done to the old city, which cannot be restored. Nevertheless, the once-magnificent city wall has now been carefully repaired, and provides a spacious and open promenade around Xi'an for both citizens and visitors to enjoy.

Xi'an has a well-developed and thriving industrial economy, which is supported by the present government. Among the most important industrial concerns are pharmaceuticals (including a joint venture factory with the Belgian company Janseen), chemicals, machinery, electrical equipment, cement, fertilizers and aviation (Boeing has set up a joint venture production plant for aircraft parts near Xi'an).

Being a provincial capital, Xi'an is also an administrative and educational centre for government services. There are several important post-secondary educational institutions including Jiaotong University and Xibei University, considered to be the finest degree granting institutions serving northwest China.

Xi'an China International Travel Service Co. Ltd.

Xi'an China International Travel Service (CITS) was founded in 1956. It is now the largest travel service among the mainland cities of China with a staff of over 500. Xi'an CITS is mainly engaged in travel industry sales and marketing promotion and in the organisation of world visitors to China. It has over 300 well-trained and professional guides fluent in various languages including English, Japanese, French, German, Spanish and Italian.

As the first agent for IATA in northwest China, Xi'an CITS also provides a complete range of services for international air-ticketing.

Since 1978 it has hosted over two million international tourists and in recent years has handled up to 200,000 visitors annually from around the globe—over 50 percent of the total number of international visitors to Shaanxi Province.

Xi'an CITS has played host to various dignitaries including the former Prime Minister of Canada Mr Pierre Trudeau and head of Microsoft Mr Bill Gates. In 1998, the company provided guides and arranged the visit of US President Mr Bill Clinton and his family to Xi'an.

The FIT (Foreign Individual Traveller) Service Centre is one of the most important departments in Xi'an CITS. The centre offers a complete and comprehensive service for individual travellers or families, organising and customising all travel arrangements to suit their specific needs.

Xi'an CITS is also experienced in organising special interest tours in such fields as calligraphy, archaeology, culture, science and technology.

Everywhere in Xi'an the visitor will find the company motto becoming a reality: *At home you are your own boss, in China your Aladdin's Lamp is CITS.*

Main Office:
48 Chang'an Road, Xi'an, China 710061
Tel. (86-29) 5262066
Fax. (86-29) 5261453; 5261558

Sales and Marketing Centre:
Tel. (86-29) 5255401
Fax. (86-29) 5261453

FIT Department:
Tel. (86-29) 5261454
Fax. (86-29) 5261454

ARTISTS AT LARGE

W e had luncheon at a restaurant in Sian—in an upstairs room reserved for foreigners, with separate tables for groups of tourists. It was a large, light, airy, rather pleasant room. Our pretty local guide, while we were still sitting at table, asked David to do a drawing of her, which he obligingly did. Within a few minutes the waiter at our table stopped serving (there was a group of French tourists at the next table who seemed to be left unattended) and was standing over David watching the progress of his work. Soon other waiters appeared and, after them, sweating and smiling, the chef. David finished his drawing. He then fished into the enormous canvas bag which Gregory always carried round and drew out his Polaroid camera. He took the guide across the dining room to a window and photographed her, setting down the portrait he had just done, on another chair beside her, for comparison. By now the whole staff of the restaurant—or of the foreigner's section of it—was clustered by the window. David took a charming photograph of the chef—wearing his white chef's cap—flanked by two assistants.

After this, even outside the restaurant in the street, where there was a small crowd awaiting us, the citizens of Sian seemed particularly friendly, as though we were three Goons arrived there. We did look rather funny: David with the flat cap he nearly always wears, even indoors, his shirt with horizontal red stripes and his different coloured socks; Gregory with his Robin Hood jerkin with a kind of cape at the back; and me with my enormous feet. The Chinese, I noticed, were always looking at my feet and politely concealing their smiles.

Stephen Spender and David Hockney, China Diary

The Little Goose Pagoda, painted by Luo Guoshi and Luo Liangbi

Facts for the Traveller

Getting to Xi'an

Before the Second World War the few foreigners who made the arduous journey to Xi'an considered themselves adventurers rather than tourists. To reach their destination they had to travel to the end of the railway line in the neighbouring province of Henan, and then transfer to bumpy carts for a further journey of six days through 'bandit infested' country. The journey became easier when the railway reached Xi'an in 1934. A new station was built only in 1986. Today Xi'an has become the main communications centre for the northwest region of China.

BY AIR

Dragonair, the Hong Kong-based airline, operates a round-trip service to Xi'an on Mondays, Wednesdays and Fridays: departing Hong Kong 8 am, arriving 10.50 am; departing Xi'an 11.50 am, arriving 2.25 pm. China Northwest Airlines, offers a service to and from Hong Kong five times a week, every Tuesday, Wednesday, Thursday, Saturday and Sunday: departing Xi'an 2.20 pm, arriving 5 pm; departing Hong Kong 6 pm, arriving 8.25 pm. There are also daily flights that connect with all major cities in China, as well as regular flights to capital cities of other southeast Asian countries.

Xi'an's airport is located in the neighbouring city of Xianyang, about 45 kilometres away. The most convenient way to reach Xi'an from Xianyang Airport is to take a taxi. Although the driver may try to negotiate the fare before departure, all taxis are fitted with meters and you should insist that this be used. As at the end of 1999, the fare into Xi'an was around Rmb 170–180 depending on the exact destination. Journey time on the expressway is around one hour—most of the time can be spent sitting in the notoriously bad traffic once in the city itself. A cheaper, slower and probably less convenient alternative is the airport bus. This makes various scheduled stops in town before terminating at the China Northwest Airlines Booking Office at Xishaomen, outside the western gate of the city (see Useful Addresses, page 153).

BY RAIL

Xi'an is on the main east-west railway that goes all the way from Shanghai to the Alataw Pass on the Xinjiang Autonomous Region border with Kazakhstan. A Eurasian railway continues to Almati, and then through several CIS republics before eventually ending up in Rotterdam.

Express trains arrive daily from Beijing (taking about 18 hours), and also from Shanghai, Chengdu, Chongqing, Guangzhou, Lanzhou, Luoyang, Nanjing, Qingdao, Taiyuan, Urumqi, and Zhengzhou. There are also numerous services to other destinations throughout China.

Hard and soft sleeper tickets can be bought in advance on the second floor of Xi'an Railway Station Ticket Office. A sign in English points the way to the special window serving foreigners, thus avoiding the need to stand in long queues with the locals downstairs. However, depending on the season it can be extremely difficult to purchase tickets, particularly during the Spring Festival (the lunar New Year holiday). To avoid potential problems and for convenience it is recommended you purchase your rail tickets through a travel service, such as CITS (see page 15). They can also provide you with accurate information on schedules.

Visas

Everyone must get a visa to go to China, but this is usually an easy, trouble-free process. Tourists travelling in a group enter China on a group visa—a single document listing all members of the group. The visa is obtained by the tour operator on behalf of the clients, and individual passports will not be stamped unless specifically requested.

Tourist visas for individual travellers can be obtained directly through Chinese embassies and consulates. Certain travel agents and tour operators around the world can also arrange individual visas. It is simplest in Hong Kong, where visas can be obtained directly from the Chinese Ministry of Foreign Affairs visa office located on the ground floor of China Resources Building, Wanchai. Just one passport photograph and a completed application form are necessary. However, they keep strict office hours and only open from Monday to Friday. A more convenient alternative is the large number of travel agents handling visa applications, or from the offices of CITS or CTS.

Visa fees vary considerably, depending on the source of the visa, and on the time taken to get it. One of the most reliable and reasonable visa services is offered by Hung Shing Travel Service to be found at Room 711, 7th floor, New East Ocean Centre, 9 Science Museum Road, Tsim Sha Tsui East, Kowloon, tel. 2369-3188, fax 2369-3293. A single-entry tourist visa costs HK$ 120 and can be issued the same day depending on the time of application. These are valid for a standard three months. Six-month multiple-entry visas can also be arranged here for about HK$ 450.

The mechanics of getting a business visa are much more flexible than in the past, particularly in Hong Kong. The applicant should have either an invitation

from the appropriate Foreign Trade Corporation (several now have permanent representatives abroad), or from the organizers of a special trade fair or seminar. In Hong Kong, all that is needed is a letter from the applicant's company confirming that he wishes to travel to China on business.

Visas can normally be extended by designated Public Security Bureaus dealing with the entry and exit of aliens. Extensions are normally granted without too much trouble for a maximum of one month, on no more than two successive occasions. The Division of Aliens and Exit-Entry Administration of the Xi'an Municipal Public Security Bureau is located close to the Bell Tower, at 138 Xi Dajie (see Useful Addresses, page 155).

Customs

The ordinary visitor is no longer required to complete a customs declaration form on arrival. There is no limit on the amount of foreign currency that can be taken in, though those holding more than US$ 5,000 (or equivalent) in cash should make a declaration. Visitors carrying goods or samples for business purposes and those with unaccompanied baggage should also make a declaration. Customs forms should be kept safely and handed in on departure.

One-and-a-half litres of alcohol over 12 percent proof, 400 cigarettes or 100 cigars, unlimited film and medicines for personal use may be brought into the country.

Antiques up to the value of Rmb 10,000 may be taken out of China as long as each article bears a red wax seal which indicates that it may be exported. Receipts for these and gold and silver goods should be kept in case inspection is required on departure.

Money

CHINESE CURRENCY

The People's Currency, or Renminbi as it is known, is the common form of exchange in China. The basic unit of currency is the *yuan*, or *kuai* as it is commonly referred to in spoken Chinese. The *yuan* is divided into 10 *jiao*, colloquially called *mao*. Each *jiao* is, in turn, divided into 10 *fen*. There are larger notes for 100, 50, 10, 5, 2 and 1 *yuan*, small notes for 5, 2 and 1 *jiao*, and coins for 5, 2 and 1 *fen*.

Hard currencies can be conveniently exchanged into Renminbi at hotels, large stores and branches of the Bank of China. All major European, American and Japanese traveller's cheques are accepted, and these are changed at a slightly better rate than cash. Renminbi can be obtained via credit card at some hotels, though a

*A common sight in the courtyards of many homes in the countryside surrounding Xi'an
—red chillies and maize drying in the autumn sunshine*

hefty surcharge is levied. The Bank of China offers the best service to holders of major credit cards subject to a minimum exchange of 1,200 Rmb.

Up to 50 percent of the total amount of Renminbi obtained may be reconverted to hard currency on leaving China, providing exchange receipts covering the amount are shown. For those travelling to Hong Kong, Renminbi can easily be converted to Hong Kong dollars at numerous money changers without the need for receipts.

FOREIGN CURRENCY

If more cash is needed during your stay, it is possible to have money wired in your name to the local main branch of the Bank of China. The remittance will arrive in four to six working days. Alternatively a substantial cash advance on your credit card can be drawn at any branch of the Bank of China. American Express cardholders many cash personal cheques up to US$ 1,000 (green/corporate card) or US$ 5,000 (gold card) every 21 days on payment of a service charge.

TRAVELLER'S CHEQUES AND CREDIT CARDS

All the usual American, European and Japanese traveller's cheques are accepted by the Bank of China and are changed at a slightly better rate than cash.

China is experiencing a credit card boom, with an estimated 100 million cards being issued by Chinese banks by the year 2000. The development should widen the use of international credit cards at retail outlets. At present international credit cards are widely accepted at designated tourist restaurants and stores as well as at most tourist hotels. However, they are of little value for most main street shopping, though they are usually accepted at the new breed of luxury stores, international boutiques and emporiums that are opening up in all the major Chinese cities.

TIPPING

Although tipping is, in theory, forbidden it has become an accepted and expected practice in many sectors of the hospitality industry. Tipping has become particularly routine in hotels. It is also becoming more prevalent in restaurants and bars frequented by foreigners or tourists, but it is not necessary where a 15 percent service charge is levied. Taxi drivers will also accept tips. For group tourists tipping of drivers and guides is an obligatory practice.

Travel Agencies and Tour Operators

There are a number of State-owned corporations which handle foreign visitors to China. The largest is China International Travel Service (CITS), see page 15. Other large organizations providing similar services are China Travel Service (CTS), China Youth Travel Service (CYTS) and Overseas Travel Corporation (OTC).

These agencies offer a comprehensive service covering accommodation, transport, food, sightseeing, interpreters, in addition to special visits to schools, hospitals, factories and other places foreigners might be interested in seeing.

Abercrombie & Kent (Hong Kong) Ltd. has been working in the People's Republic of China since 1983. They operate both set brochure tours of China (published out of London, England and the United States) as well as handle personally tailored China itineraries for both groups and individual travellers. A & K has built up a strong network of contacts within China (including Xi'an) which can result in arrangements not always possible to the individual traveller or group tours operated by other companies. This includes a good working relationship with the Cultural Relics Bureau and the archaeology authorities of Shaanxi Province. With a regional office in Hong Kong, A & K offers personal on-site service to Xi'an and other areas of China. (For contact details see Useful Addresses section on page 153)

Local Time

Amazingly for a country measuring some 4,300 kilometres (over 2,500 miles) from east to west, the whole of China operates within one time zone, eight hours ahead of GMT and 13 hours ahead of EST. There is no daylight saving time in China.

Communications

Direct Dialling for calls within China and International Direct Dialling is available in nearly all tourist hotels. The same hotels also have business centres providing photocopying, telex and facsimile services. Internet and e-mailing services are fast becoming common as well. Public phones on the streets of large cities are increasing becoming card operated—phone cards can be purchased from your hotel or from numerous small general shops and stalls. Be aware that phone charges begin when the phone rings and not when it is answered, so payment must still be made even if there is no answer.

China's own English-language newspaper, China Daily, is available at most hotels, and the larger joint-venture hotels usually have available a selection of international papers such as International Herald Tribune, Asian Wall Street Journal, USA Today and South China Morning Post, although these will obviously be a day or two late.

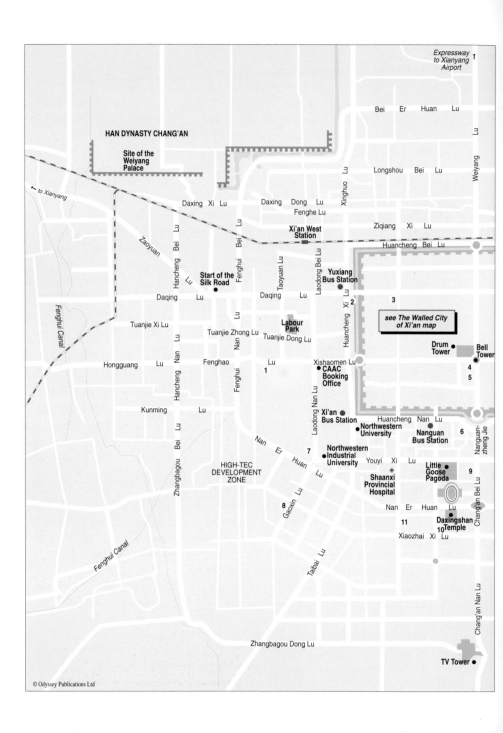

Expressway
to Xianyang
Airport

HAN DYNASTY CHANG'AN

Site of the
Weiyang
Palace

← to Xianyang

Bei   Er   Huan   Lu

Weiyang   Lu

Longshou   Bei   Lu

Daxing   Xi   Lu   Daxing   Dong   Lu
Fenghe Lu

Xinghuo   Lu

Ziqiang   Xi   Lu

Xi'an West
Station

Huancheng   Bei   Lu

Zaoyuan

Hancheng   Bei   Lu

Fenghui   Bei   Lu

Taoyuan   Lu

Laodong Bei Lu

Yuxiang
Bus Station

Start of the
Silk Road

Daqing   Lu

Fenghui   Lu

Daqing   Lu

Huancheng   Xi   Lu

2

3

see The Walled City
of Xi'an map

Tuanjie Xi Lu

Hancheng   Nan   Lu

Tuanjie Zhong Lu   Tuanjie Dong Lu

Labour
Park

Drum
Tower

Bell
Tower

Fenghao

Fenghui   Lu

1

Xishaomen Lu

4

Hongguang   Lu

CAAC
Booking
Office

5

Fenghui Canal

Kunming   Lu

Laodong Nan Lu

Xi'an
Bus Station

Huancheng   Nan   Lu

Zhangbagou   Bei   Lu

Northwestern
University

Nanguan
Bus Station

6

Nanguan-
zheng Jie

7

Northwestern
Industrial
University

Youyi   Xi   Lu

Nan   Er   Huan   Lu

Little
Goose
Pagoda

9

HIGH-TEC
DEVELOPMENT
ZONE

Gaoxin   Lu

Shaanxi
Provincial
Hospital

Chang'an Bei Lu

8

Nan   Er   Huan   Lu

11

Daxingshan
Temple

10

Xiaozhai   Xi   Lu

Taibai   Lu

Fenghui Canal

Chang'an Nan Lu

Zhangbagou Dong Lu

TV Tower

© Odyssey Publications Ltd

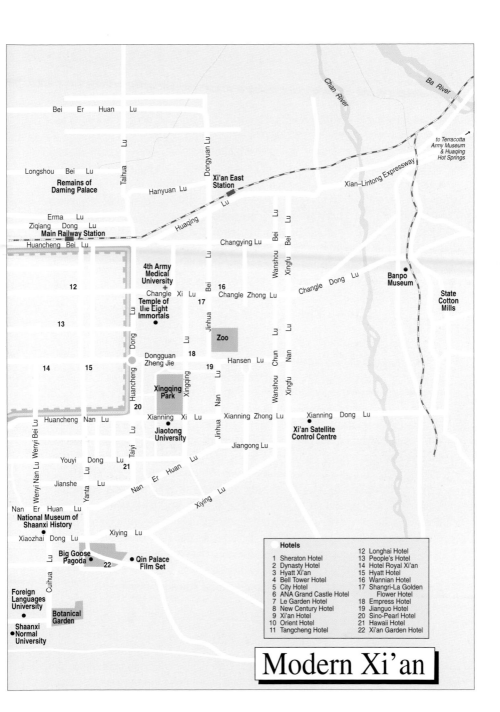

Bei Er Huan Lu

Longshou Bei Lu
Remains of Daming Palace

Erma Lu
Ziqiang Dong Lu
Main Railway Station
Huancheng Bei Lu

Taihua Lu

Hanyuan Lu

Huaqing Lu

Dongyuan Lu

Xi'an East Station

Lu

Changying Lu

Chan River

Ba River

to Terracotta Army Museum & Huaqing Hot Springs

Xian–Lintong Expressway

12

4th Army Medical University

Changle Xi Lu
Temple of the Eight Immortals

13

14   **15**

Dong Lu

Huancheng Dong Lu

Dongguan Zheng Jie

Xingqing Park

20

Huancheng Nan Lu

Jinhua Lu

Changle Zhong Lu

16

17

Zoo

18

Hansen Lu

19

Xingqing Lu

Nan Lu

Xianning Xi Lu

Xianning Zhong Lu

Jiaotong University

Jiangong Lu

Wanshou Bei Lu

Xingfu Bei Lu

Chun Nan Lu

Wanshou Nan Lu

Xingfu Nan Lu

Changle Dong Lu

Banpo Museum

State Cotton Mills

Xianning Dong Lu

Xi'an Satellite Control Centre

Jinhua Lu

Wenyi Nan Lu   Wenyi Bei Lu

Youyi Dong Lu

Jianshe Lu

Taiyi Lu

Yanta Lu

21

Nan Er Huan Lu

Xiying Lu

Nan Er Huan Lu
National Museum of Shaanxi History
Xiaozhai Dong Lu

Cuihua Lu

Xiying Lu

Big Goose Pagoda

22

Qin Palace Film Set

Foreign Languages University

Botanical Garden

Shaanxi Normal University

Hotels

1 Sheraton Hotel
2 Dynasty Hotel
3 Hyatt Xi'an
4 Bell Tower Hotel
5 City Hotel
6 ANA Grand Castle Hotel
7 Le Garden Hotel
8 New Century Hotel
9 Xi'an Hotel
10 Orient Hotel
11 Tangcheng Hotel

12 Longhai Hotel
13 People's Hotel
14 Hotel Royal Xi'an
15 Hyatt Hotel
16 Wannian Hotel
17 Shangri-La Golden
   Flower Hotel
18 Empress Hotel
19 Jianguo Hotel
20 Sino-Pearl Hotel
21 Hawaii Hotel
22 Xi'an Garden Hotel

Modern Xi'an

Packing Checklist

As well as bringing along any prescription medicines you may need, it is a good idea to pack a supply of common cold and stomach remedies. While it is not necessary to pack toilet paper these days, it is advisable to take some with you when going out sightseeing, as public toilets do not always provide it. Bring plenty of film for your camera and batteries for this and any other accessories you may be carrying. Although both are widely available, they could be old stock or of dubious quality. Comfortable, non-slip shoes for walking are a must.

The electricity supply is 220 volts and hotels have a wide variety of socket types, though many provide adaptors for British and American plugs.

If you wear glasses or contact lenses bring your prescription and a spare pair, and ensure you are well-stocked with essential fluids and solutions.

Health

There are no mandatory vaccination requirements. However, you may be advised by your doctor to take certain precautions. In recent years the US Consulate in Hong Kong has recommended inoculations against hepatitis A and B, Japanese encephalitis B, tetanus, polio, cholera and malaria. The risk of contracting any of these diseases is small, although it increases during the summer months and in rural areas. To minimize risks, remember to drink only mineral or boiled water—the former is sold almost everywhere and the latter is provided in flasks in all hotel rooms and from carriage attendants on board trains. Make sure food is freshly cooked and peel all fruit.

A word of caution, too, for those suffering from asthma or other respiratory problems: as China continues to industrialize at pace, and the improved average standard of living means that the bicycle is now increasingly outnumbered on the streets of major cities by the motorbike, private car and taxi, the quality of air in places like Xi'an can sometimes be quite shocking. This can of course vary with the weather conditions, but in the dry autumn months, particularly when farmers burn off their fields after the harvest, air pollution can be considerable.

Holidays

In contrast to the long calendar of traditional Chinese festivals, modern China now has only four official holidays: New Year's Day (1st January); Labour Day (1st May);

National Day, marking the foundation of the People's Republic of China (1st October); and Chinese New Year, usually called Spring Festival in China itself, which comes at the lunar new year, usually around the end of January or beginning of February.

Climate and Clothing

Xi'an's climate is much drier and cooler than that of southwest or southeast China, and less extreme than that of Beijing. In American terms, the climate is similar to that of Wyoming. The Qinling Mountains to the south of the Wei River valley shield Xi'an from the southeastern monsoon, which brings much rain and considerable humidity to the neighbouring province of Sichuan. Annual precipitation is only 530–600 millimetres (21–24 inches). Most of the rainfall occurs in July, August and September.

Spring is usually the best season, with the city at its most beautiful under relatively clear skies. Summer begins in May, and is usually fine and sunny. The hottest month is July, when noon temperatures may reach over 38°C (100°F). Late summer and early autumn is cooler and can be overcast. Late autumn is usually fine, and winter is dry and cold with a little snow. At night during winter temperatures usually drop well below 0°C (32°F).

In mid-summer only the lightest clothing is necessary. In mid-winter thermal underwear and multi-layered clothing add to comfort.

XI'AN TEMPERATURES

	Average	High	Low		Average	High	Low
Jan	−1.3°C (29°F)	5.1°C (41°F)	−5.5°C (22°F)	Jul	26.7°C (80°F)	34.0°C (93°F)	22.5°C (72°F)
Feb	2.1°C (36°F)	8.0°C (46°F)	−2.4°C (28°F)	Aug	25.4°C (78°F)	31.5°C (89°F)	20.9°C (70°F)
Mar	8.0°C (46°F)	14.7°C (58°F)	2.7°C (37°F)	Sep	19.4°C (67°F)	25.0°C (77°F)	15.5°C (60°F)
Apr	14.0°C (57°F)	21.5°C (70°F)	8.6°C (47°F)	Oct	13.6°C (56°F)	20.0°C (68°F)	8.9°C (48°F)
May	19.2°C (67°F)	27.7°C (82°F)	13.8°C (57°F)	Nov	6.5°C (44°F)	12.4°C (54°F)	2.3°C (36°F)
Jun	25.3°C (78°F)	32.8°C (91°F)	19.0°C (66°F)	Dec	0.6°C (33°F)	6.2°C (43°F)	−3.9°C (25°F)

Getting around Xi'an

There are some fascinating areas within the city walls which are well worth exploring on foot. Particularly attractive for their old buildings are the streets around the Drum Tower and the Great Mosque as well as those near the South and West Gates and north and west of the Beilin Museum. Dong Dajie, the main shopping area, is another good place to stroll, with its large department stores and wide sidewalks. Xi Dajie is more compact and has dozens of small shops with a variety of intriguing items.

Public transport is cheap but could prove difficult unless you have your destination written in Chinese or a basic knowledge of the language. If you plan to venture out independently, it is always a good idea to ask your hotel receptionist to write the names of the places you intend to visit in Chinese characters to assist in using public transport or just asking directions on the street.

There are numerous bus routes around the city, some of which extend into the newly developed urban areas. Buses can be an interesting way to get around, but are often comparatively slow and very crowded. Excellent maps of Xi'an are available from hotel shops and from hawkers at the railway station, bus stations and most sightseeing spots and these clearly show all bus routes, the bus numbers and where they terminate. These are very useful and although most of them are in Chinese, some are printed with names in English as well.

Taxis are available at hotels, can be hailed in the streets, and usually wait at all the major places of interest to tourists. Literally hundreds of small red Chinese-made taxis crowd the streets of Xi'an, and one only has to stand on the second-floor balcony of the Bell Tower at the centre of town to appreciate just how many. They have a 5 yuan flag fall and charge 1.20 yuan per kilometre thereafter, thereby making them a convenient and affordable means of getting around town. All taxis are fitted with meters and drivers generally use them without having to be asked (the airport is perhaps the only exception to this).

If you prefer to cycle around Xi'an, you can rent a bicycle from one of the bicycle rental shops in the city centre. One convenient location is near the gate of the People's Hotel, where there are a few small shops.

Many of Xi'an's major sights are a long way from the city, but CITS and other travel agencies offer tours by comfortable air-conditioned buses to most of these places. Tours can also be easily arranged at all major hotels. Public buses go to most sightseeing places as well.

Those who prefer to arrange their own itinerary can hire a taxi for the day, or customized tour through the FITS department of CITS (see page 15). With your

The Walled City of Xi'an

© Odyssey Publications Ltd

Railway Station

Jiefang Hotel

Bank of China

Long Distance Bus Station

Eighth Route Army Office Museum

Revolution Park

People's Stadium

People's Hotel

Provincial Government Building

Night Market

Hyatt Hotel

Royal Hotel

Temple of the Recumbent Dragon

Forest of Steles Museum

Telegraph & Telephone Building

Main Post Office

Train Ticket Advance Booking

Lianhu Park

Drum Tower
Drum Tower Square

Bell Tower

Bell Tower Hotel

Great Mosque

Temple of the Town God

Grand New World Hotel

Children's Park

Guangren Temple

Beimen (North gate)

Dongmen (East gate)

Nanmen (South gate)

Ximen (West gate)

Hongguang Gate

Heping Gate

Jianguomen

Dongshunchengjie Beiduan
Dongshunchengjie Nanduan

Dong 8-Lu
Dong 7-Lu
Dong 7-9-Lu
Shangjie Lu
Shangjian Lu
Dong 5-Lu
Dong 4-Lu
Dong 3-Lu
Dong 2-Lu
Dong 1-Lu
Shangqin

Shangjian Lu
Dong Lu
Jiefang Lu
Jiefang Jie

Jianguo Lu

Xi 8-Lu
Xi 7-9 Jie
Shangde Jie
Xi 4-Lu
Xi 3-Lu
Xi 2-Lu
Xi 1-Lu
Shangde Lu
Dongxin Jie

Beishunchengjie Dongduan
Bei Xin Jie
Xi 7-Lu
Xi 5-Lu

Xinmin Jie

Xixin Jie
Bei Dajie

Naxin Jie

Luoma Shi
Dongmutou Shi
Dongtingmen
Duanlumen
Dongcangmen
Machangzi
Xiamaling
Kaifang Xiang
Juhuayuan

Nan Dajie
Zhuba Shi
Fen Xiang
Naryuanmen
Nanguangi Jie
Wuxing Jie
Yandian Jie
Dajie

Culture Street
Sanwe Jie
Deju Xiang
Dacheja Xiang
Daboli Xiang
Dongsheng Jie

Beishunchengjie Xiduan
Tangfang Jie
Weimin Xiang
Qingnian Lu
Bayi Jie
Lianhu Lu
Xibei 3-Lu
Xibei 2-Lu
Xibei 1-Lu
Xiwuyuan
Dongmeng Xiang
Nanndao Xiang

Erfu Jie
Hongbu Jie
Xiaopiyuan Jie
Dapiyuan
Xihuamen
Beiyuanmen
Xiyangshi Jie
Huajue Xiang
Beiguanli Jie
Guangming Xiang
Miaohou Jie
Daxuexi Xiang
Damaishi Jie
Xi Dajie
Bemdao Xiang
Shuangrenfu

Sajinqiao

own transport and an early start it is possible to visit Famen Temple, and the tombs of Qian Ling in a single day trip. Another worthwhile day trip can take in the Xianyang museum, and the tombs of Mao Ling and Zhao Ling.

Shopping

Earlier this century Xi'an was known for its curio shops stocked with antiquities of the city. Today, however, you would be lucky to find anything very old; most antiques in these shops date from the Qing and Republican periods, or are reproductions.

Shaanxi's folk crafts are thriving with the rapid increase of tourism in Xi'an. Hawkers cluster round every site visited by tourists, selling brightly coloured patchwork waistcoats and shoulder bags, embroidered children's shoes, hats and toys, shadow puppets, and amusing painted clay ornaments decorated in brilliant primary colours. Buying in the free markets can be much more fun than in the established arts and crafts shops, but be prepared for some fierce bargaining, and even then you may not be assured of a good deal. It always pays to shop around— many is the occasion that the unwary tourist has returned with their purchase only to find the same item on sale in the hotel gift shop for considerably less.

Embroidery is one of Shaanxi's richest traditional skills that is gaining recognition elsewhere; some of the more distinctive items crop up in hotel souvenir shops in other parts of China. There are children's patchwork waistcoats, predominantly red, and decorated with some, or all, of the 'five poisonous creatures'—toad, snake, centipede, lizard, scorpion—in the belief that the process of sewing the forms on to the waistcoat will nullify the creatures' evil powers. Embroidered cylindrical cotton pillows, with an intricately decorated tiger's head at each end, are also common. These are favourite gifts to babies when the first month of life is celebrated. Tiger motifs often appear on other children's clothes and shoes, since the tiger can readily devour evil spirits. Its eyes are usually wide open and staring to help deflect evil influences away from the wearer.

Painted clay toys, originally from the nearby city of Fengxiang, in western Shaanxi Province, were traditional gifts for festivals, weddings and birthdays. They can now be bought in many of the free markets and souvenir shops in the city. These toys are often in the form of tigers, sometimes covered with flowers or butterflies, and are predominantly red and green to symbolize prosperity and happiness. Other popular subjects are comical monkeys and chubby children.

Shadow puppets, cut out of semi-transparent hide and painted in bright colours, are another speciality of Xi'an. The puppet's flexible joints allow it—in skilled hands at least—to somersault expertly, or engage in armed combat. The characters depicted are usually from traditional folk tales.

Chinese stone rubbings are a very appropriate souvenir of China's former capital since Xi'an has the country's best collection of steles, or inscribed stone tables, most of them in the Forest of Steles Museum (see page 117). The rubbings of memorials, calligraphy, pictures and even maps are produced by laying paper on top of a stele, and then pounding it with ball of tightly-wrapped ink-filled cloth. It is often possible to see this being done, either at the Forest of Steles or at a handicraft factory. An expert job from a famous stone can cost hundreds, even thousands, of yuan. Rubbings of all prices are on sale almost everywhere around the city.

You may find it interesting to visit the workshops and showrooms of some small handicraft enterprises. Quality varies; none of the factories are particularly old but some of the craft techniques are worth seeing, and you will always be given a warm welcome. The Jade Carving Factory of Xi'an is at 173 Xiyi Lu, and has a retail outlet. Some 300 workers carve jadeite, amethyst, crystal, many other semi-precious stones and petrified wood. Attached to the factory is a unit making rubbings from reproductions of stones in the Forest of Steles Museum.

The Xi'an Special Arts and Crafts Factory on Huancheng Xi Lu, just north of the West Gate, produces sculptures and collage pictures using sea-shells, feathers, silk and other material together with inlaid woodwork.

Other interesting items found most easily at the small shops surrounding major sights include local pottery for everyday use, basketware, papercuts, and micro-carvings on minute pieces of ivory no bigger than a grain of rice.

Many tourist shops sell Chinese paintings and calligraphy. Most of the work is by mediocre local artists, of which there are literally scores. The city's most famous artists are Luo Guoshi and his son Luo Liangbi, who specialize in painting local scenic spots (see page 17).

Another popular local art form are the colourful paintings of the peasant farmers of Huxian (see page 136). A good selection of these for sale can be found at the Little Goose Pagoda and the shop of the Tang Dynasty Arts Museum, just around the corner from the Big Goose Pagoda. The latter also has a good selection of shadow puppets.

Tourists or visitors planning to make serious purchases of local arts or crafts would be well advised to visit the Wenbaozhai Store on Yanta Zhong Lu. This is a Tourist Administration appointed store selling locally made silk carpets, jade, pottery, furniture and art. The store prides itself on its honesty and claims to be cheaper than anywhere else in town, promising to match any lower prices found elsewhere. Here buyers can be assured of purchasing the genuine article as all items come with a certificate of authenticity. The reproduction terracotta warriors on sale here are made in the only factory authorized to use the original Gaoling County clay. There are also some workshops for display only, where visitors can watch craftsmen and women carving jade and making pottery or carpets. The store can arrange for shipping and insurance and accepts all major currencies and credit cards. It is open daily from 8.30 am to 6 pm.

Replicas of the distinctive Banpo pottery can be bought at the Banpo Museum Retail Shop.

The main shopping street is Dong Dajie, particularly the section between Nanxin Jie and the Bell Tower. The principal department store, the Xi'an Kaiyuan Shopping Centre, is located opposite the Bell Tower on the south side of Dong Dajie. This state-owned store is one of the newest in Xi'an and seems to stock everything imaginable, from microwaves to washing machines and food to fashion. It is interesting to visit if only to see what is available to the newly-affluent middle class of China. On the opposite side of the Bell Tower, beneath the square on the north

Shaanxi shadow puppet

side of Xi Dajie, is the expensive Century Ginwa Department Store, stocking all the latest European fashion labels.

In complete contrast to these is the street market of Luoma Shi. This used to be where mules and horses were sold in ancient times, but the street has now become the biggest clothing market in Xi'an with cheap fashion from the export-orientated garment factories of the Special Economic Zones of Guangdong. A little farther along Dong Dajie are the Foreign Languages Bookshop, the Xinhua Bookshop (for publications in Chinese). There are also restaurants, snack-bars and fruit and vegetable stalls.

Another important shopping area is around Jiefang Lu, within the northeast corner of the walled city.

On Xi Dajie, and of particular interest to visitors, are many small Chinese opera costume shops supplying the municipal and county opera troupes of Shaanxi Province with embroidered silk costumes, elaborate head-dresses, hats, false beards and whiskers and odd props.

A fascinating, Qing-dynasty style Ancient Culture Street located next to the Forest of Steles Museum, has many calligraphy and painting stores, cloisonné stores and folk art stores. Most items on sale tend to be cheap reproductions, but the street itself is interesting to see.

(above) Child's appliquéd vest featuring four of the 'five poisonous creatures'. (below) Fengxiang County painted clay tiger

Food and Drink

In Xi'an the fare is generally plain and provincial, although good food is available if you search it out. The cooking offered by small street-side restaurants can sometimes be better, and certainly cheaper, than that offered by some hotel restaurants. However, the top-flight hotels around town now offer some excellent cuisine, both Western and Asian.

In country areas of Shaanxi Province (of which Xi'an is the capital) noodles and steamed bread are more popular than rice, which is the staple in southern China. Eating habits throughout the northwest of China have been strongly influenced by the Hui, Chinese-speaking Muslims who of course do not eat pork. Therefore mutton is an important source of protein in the region. Muslim food can be sampled at the stalls around the Drum Tower, especially in the early evening. The best-known, best-loved dish is call *kaoyangrou*, spicy barbecued mutton on skewers. Boiled mutton ravioli served in spicy sauce, *yangrou suantang shuijiao*, sold by the bowl, can be found in the same area. This is a particularly delicious and filling meal which can be served with or without chilli depending on your preference.

Another popular local dish, also Hui in origin, is the hearty *yangrou paomo*. A big bowl and two large baked flatbreads are provided. The customer breaks the bread into very small pieces and takes the bowl back to the kitchen where a mutton and vegetable soup, with noodles, is poured over the broken pieces of bread. It is difficult to describe the taste—perhaps something like haggis stew, noodles and digestive biscuits come closest to it!

At a relatively more sophisticated level, Xi'an has its own special delicacies served in some of the larger restaurants. Banquets start with a cold plate of *hors d'oeuvres* arranged in the shape of a phoenix, peacock or butterfly. Other dishes include fish in milk soup, served in a copper chafing dish (*guozi yu*), coin-shaped egg and hair vegetables (*jinqian facai*), sliced pig tripe and duck gizzard (*cuan shuang cui*), whole crispy 'calabash' chicken (*hulu ji*) and braised quail (*tiepa anchun*). Chinese wolfberry and white fungus in soup (*goupi dun yiner*) is a tonic, particularly good for the lungs.

Sweet dishes offered in ordinary restaurants tend to be sugary, starchy and filled with red bean, peanuts or baihe, lily bulb. A number of different cakes and biscuits are on sale, including crystal cakes (*shuijing bing*) and egg-thread cakes (*dansi bing*).

The leading brand of liqueur is call 'Xifeng', a colourless spirit made in Liulin Village, near Fengxiang, about 145 kilometres (90 miles) west of Xi'an. Another local drink is the yellow Osmanthus Thick Wine (*Huanggui choujiu*). Both are said to owe their origin to alcoholic drinks of the Tang period. There two main local bottled beer, Baoji and Hans. The latter is produced in a 'light' or 'dry' variety by the largest brewery in Xi'an—a joint-venture with a German company.

There is a snack street in Dongxin Jie in the east of the walled city which is particularly lively after dark. One side of the street serves Chinese food and the other specializes in Muslim cooking. *Yangrou suantang shuijiao* is also available here. Such delicacies can be enjoyed at Muslim establishments which usually display a mirror inscribed with a pot and Arabic script (the pot being a symbol of Muslim cleanliness as it holds water for washing hands).

Entertainment and the Arts

Xi'an is the home of several professional performing arts organizations serving both the city and the countryside. The city also has its own Conservatory of Music (at Daxingshan Temple Park), a provincial Opera School attached to the Institute of Opera in Wenyi Lu, and its own film studio (see page 37) near the Big Goose Pagoda.

The Shaanxi Acrobatics Troupe, which includes conjurors, is very popular with local people. The Shaanxi Song and Dance Troupe is known for its vocal, orchestral and instrumental performances of both Chinese and Western music, including Western light classical, international folk and Chinese operatic pieces. The Xi'an Song and Dance Troupe concentrates on Western ballet and Chinese traditional dance. Like the Shaanxi Troupe it has its own orchestra.

There are several big theatres in the city. The most important is the People's Theatre on Bei Dajie. This is mainly used for concerts, dancing and Beijing opera (performed by the Shaanxi Number One and Shaanxi Number Two Opera Companies).

China has over 300 forms of local theatre and the celebrated local Qinqiang opera of Shaanxi Province is one of the oldest, most vigorous and most influential of them all. It is almost certainly the original form of 'clapper opera', with which it is synonymous. In this style of Chinese opera, time is beaten with large wooden clap boards that look like oversize castanets.

The drama is performed in local Xi'an dialect, with its own characteristic, rather loud, vocal style, accompanied by string instruments. It has its own conventions of costumes and make-up. Individual operas are often three or four hours long with rapidly developing plots using all the dramatic devices found in Shakespearean comedies—abrupt changes in fortune, mistaken identities, men dressed as women, women dressed as men, both as animals (notably predatory, acrobatic tigers). Drag parts in which comedians take off vulgar, meddlesome old ladies are often star roles.

Poster for the film Judou, *directed by Zhang Yimou*

XI'AN FILM STUDIO

In 1985 a Chinese movie, *Yellow Earth*, was hailed as the most imaginative and original film shown at the London Film Festival that year. *Yellow Earth's* beautifully shot scenes of the loess landscape of Shaanxi, its innovative use of imagery and the bold political stance implicit in its theme of remorselessly unchanging peasant attitudes promised an exciting breakthrough in Chinese cinema. This has not quite happened, although, for a time, there was a remarkable concentration of creative film directors in Xi'an.

Xi'an Film Studio, established in 1956, is housed in a group of semi-derelict warehouses on Xiying Lu near the Big Goose Pagoda—a good view of the site can be gained from the top of the Qin Palace film set.

Several of the so-called 'Fifth Generation' of film-makers (post-Cultural Revolution graduates of the Beijing Film Academy) flocked there in the early 1980s. Chen Kaige, the director of *Yellow Earth*, and Zhang Yimou, its cinematographer, both worked in Xi'an, although neither was officially employed by the city's film studio. During that period, the head of Xi'an Film Studio was Wu Tianming, and it was he who gave the young directors the support and encouragement to break out of the mould: while the studio continued to produce popular or politically correct films, it sponsored a few on the basis of their artistic potential rather than their mass appeal or propagandist content. Several of the pictures, after long deliberation by Chinese censors, secured international release. These include *Life*, based on a novella by Shaanxi-born writer Lu Yao; *River Without Buoys* (by the same director, Wu Tianming); *Wild Mountain*, directed by Yan Xueshu; *Big Parade* (directed by Chen Kaige, with Zhang Yimou as cinematographer); and *The Black Cannon Incident*, directed by Huang Jianxin.

Wu Tianming and Chen Kaige have since moved to the United States, but Zhang Yimou has remained in Xi'an, where he grew up. In recent years Zhang has become Xi'an Film Studio's most famous son, making a series of movies which have attracted a great deal of attention from world cinema circles. After making his debut as a director with *Red Sorghum* (voted best picture at the Berlin Festival), he has directed *Judou* (first Chinese film to be nominated for an Oscar), *Raise the Red Lantern* and *The Story of Qiu Ju* (winner of the Golden Lion Award at the Venice Film Festival in 1992). Zhang recently added to these awards, winning a second Golden Lion at the 1999 Venice Film Festival with *Not One Less*. Part of the charm of this moving film, based on a true story about a 13-year-old primary school teacher, lies in the performances of its cast of non-professional children whose natural reactions were captured by hidden cameras.

Unfortunately, in the fast-changing China of the 1990s, Qinqiang is losing its popularity, especially amongst young people. The two Qinqiang companies have been forced to spend most of their year touring the countryside, where the farming communities still enjoy live operas. If you are interested, you should ask your guide or hotel to check to find out when performances are scheduled in the city and if so, where you can buy tickets.

The Tang Dynasty is a theatre and restaurant that offers dinner followed by a one-hour performance by the Tang Dynasty Song and Dance Troupe, attempting to reproduce authentic music and dance of the ancient capital Chang'an. This colourful and lively performance features musical instruments usually seen only in museums and no longer used by modern-day orchestras. The theatre can seat up to 500 diners for the evening performance and booking is advisable. Dinner begins at 7 pm. During the peak season an earlier matinee performance without the meal begins at 5.45 pm. The theatre offers a lunchtime buffet but this is without the show. (See page 150 for more details.)

Flora and Fauna

During the Tang dynasty (AD 618–907) horticulture flourished in the capital Chang'an (present day Xi'an). One of its citizens was the most celebrated gardener of Chinese history, the hunchback 'Camel' Guo. He is supposed to have grown golden peaches and propagated lotus with deep blue flowers by soaking the seeds in indigo dye.

The inhabitants of the capital were especially proud of their tree peonies, which became something of a mania, and blooms were sold for huge sums in the Chang'an Flower Market. The most popular colours were pale pink and deep purple. Tree peonies had been cultivated from about the fifth century onwards, originally in either Shaanxi or Sichuan. (The plant did not reach Europe until 1789 when the first one was found a home in London's Kew Gardens). The best peony garden was at Da Cien Temple, the temple of the Big Goose Pagoda (see page 95). It is no longer there today, but the Xi'an Botanical Garden has a small display. While perhaps not worth a special trip, the Botanical Garden is an excellent place to escape the crowds that fill most tourist sights and is a short taxi ride from the Big Goose Pagoda or Daxingshan Temple. It has a good variety of trees and plants in peaceful surroundings and, depending on the season, can be quite pretty. It is located on Cuihua Lu, south of the city, and can be reached by bus number 27 or by taxi.

In the second century BC, an envoy of Emperor Han Wudi (reigned 140–86 BC), who was sent to central Asia, brought the pomegranate tree back to China. Today, during the months of May and June, the hillsides around Lintong County, including the slopes of the Mausoleum of the First Emperor of Qin, are covered with the red and white pomegranate flowers. The fruit grown in Xi'an and especially Lintong, 15 kilometres (9 miles) to the east, is considered the best in the country, giving rise to the Chinese saying that 'When you think of Lintong, you think of pomegranates.'

The first attempt to catalogue the animals, birds and reptiles of Shaanxi according to Western science was made in 1908–9. Robert Stirling Clark of New York led an expedition of 36 men, including the ornithologist Arthur de C Sowerby of the Smithsonian.

Among some of today's rarest birds recorded by Sowerby were the pink, grey and white 'Chinese' ibises. These wading birds, members of the stork family, are properly called Japanese ibis, though they are call toki in Japan. The long-beaked birds are distinguished by the bright red colouring on the side of the head and legs. The adult grows to a length of about 77 centimetres (2.5 feet) head to tail.

These ibises were formerly spread throughout east and northeast China, Korea and Japan, but environmental changes in the 20th century have been disastrous for the species. They declined in numbers and disappeared altogether after 1964. By 1980 there were only two known pairs left in the world. These were at the Toki Protection Centre on Japan's Sado Island. They had not reproduced for four years, and artificial incubation failed. Then, that same year, Chinese zoologists found two nesting pairs in Shaanxi, at Yangxian County in the Qinling Mountains. Three young were hatched that year in what is now the Qinling Number One Ibis Colony.

By comparison with the ibis, the giant panda is not nearly so rare. There are still about 1,000 of these large black and white, high-altitude living, bamboo-munching 'cat-bears'. Most of them are in the neighbouring province of Sichuan; a few unlucky, if pampered, ones play star roles in world zoos. In Shaanxi Province there is one special nature reserve for them in Foping County, southwest of Xi'an and not far from the Qinling Ibis Colony.

The orange snub-nosed monkey, also known as the golden-haired monkey, is another inhabitant of the Qinling Mountains. Found in birch forests and mountain gullies, at around 2,500–3,000 metres (about 8,000–10,000 feet), these very agile, acrobatic animals have bright yellow-orange fur, with white chests, long tails and distinctive blue circles around their eyes.

The so-called Reeves pheasant is the original proud possessor of the long, waving tail feathers worn by generals in Chinese opera. The tail of the male reaches to 100–140 centimetres (3.3–4.6 feet) in length. The bird is found in mountain forests, between 600-2,000 metres (about 2,000–5,000 feet) above sea level.

The Xi'an Zoo on Jinhua Beilu, not far from the Shangri-La Golden Flower Hotel, has examples of both giant and lesser pandas, together with the what is said to be the only surviving brown panda in the world. There are also pheasants and orange snub-nosed monkeys as well as northeast China tigers, leopards, Sichuan parrots, wild donkeys and other animals indigenous to China. There are also a number of animals presented to the Xi'an Zoo by the Japanese cities of Kyoto and Nara, with which Xi'an has a formal as well as a historical relationship. The zoo was established in Revolution Park in 1956, but moved to its much larger present site to the east in 1976.

Until surveys are published of the complete fauna of southern Shaanxi there will not be a definitive inventory of species. The British traveller, Violet Cressy-Marcks, who interviewed Mao Zedong in Yan'an, recorded in 1938 that in an area 20 miles from the city she saw 'common jay, Chinese jay, blue magpie, golden eagle, pheasants, green woodpeckers, flocks of bustard, wild horned sheep and wild ducks and I was told there were leopards but I did not see any.' Near Xi'an 'there were many sulphur bellied rats, wood and field mice, also mallard, teal, wrens, redstarts, minks and goral'. At Lintong she saw 'geese, ducks, hares, snipe, bustard and mallard'. The wildlife of the Wei River plain is almost certainly much depleted now, in contrast to that of the mountains of the south.

An earthenware pot excavated from the Neolithic site at Banpo displaying a typical fish design.
Just one of a wide variety of pots on display at the National Museum of Shaanxi History and the
Banpo Museum itself with the characteristic bold designs and abstract patterns
of the Yangshao Culture from about 6,000 years ago

Places of Interest in the Xi'an Area

Period One: Pre-Qin

Background

Xi'an lies a few miles south of the Wei River, a western tributary of the Yellow River. Near the modern city is the ancient site of Chang'an (Everlasting Peace), which served as the capital of several ruling dynasties spanning a period of over 1,000 years. But the Wei valley had been settled much earlier. In fact, both the Wei valley and Shaanxi Province are traditionally known as one of the 'cradles' of Chinese civilization. The Yellow Emperor—the mythical ancestor and first sovereign of the Han race who is said to have lived in the third millennium BC—has his legendary burial place at Huangling, a town halfway between Xi'an and Yan'an in northern Shaanxi.

PALAEOLITHIC

Before the present landscape of the Wei valley was created from deposits of sand blown from the Mongolian Plateau, man's early ancestors lived in the area. Between 1963 and 1966 a skull (now in Beijing), jaw and various other bones of Lantian Man, a form of *Homo erectus* dating from around 800,000 BC, were discovered 38 kilometres (24 miles) southwest of Xi'an.

A bronze vessel of the Western Zhou dynasty

In the spring of 1978 another startling discovery was made in Dali County, to the east of Xi'an near the provincial border with Shanxi: an almost complete skull of what is now known as Dali Man. He is thought to belong to an early subspecies of *Homo sapiens*, living in perhaps 300,000 or 200,000 BC.

NEOLITHIC

The development of agriculture found an ideal setting in the Wei and middle Yellow river valleys, with their deep loess deposits containing all the necessary minerals for successful cultivation. From approximately 5000 BC onwards settlements were formed, larger and more permanent than similar ones elsewhere in the world. The early Neolithic stage in China is called Yangshao Culture. The name Painted Pottery Culture is sometimes preferred, which contrasts with the Black Pottery, or Longshan Culture which followed it. Yangshao Culture lasted until 3000 BC. A typical Yangshao or Painted Pottery Culture settlement has been excavated at Banpo, on the outskirts of Xi'an.

Sights

BANPO MUSEUM

In 1953 when workers were laying the foundations for a factory at Banpo, less than seven kilometres (four miles) east of Xi'an, they came upon the remains of an ancient settlement. The discovery of this New Stone Age village has been described as the 'greatest single contribution to prehistoric archaeology in east Asia' (John Hay, *Ancient China*). Dating from approximately 5000 to 4000 BC, it is the most complete example of an agricultural Neolithic settlement anywhere in the world. Its remarkably well-preserved condition makes it a major attraction for visitors to Xi'an.

An area of 4,000 square metres (one acre) has been fully excavated, enclosed and put on view to the public. Foundations of 45 houses have been uncovered, some round, some square. The largest dwelling may have been a communal meeting place, or alternatively the house of the chief. Among the other impressive finds are: 200 storage pots, a collection of pottery and tools, a pottery-making centre and a graveyard with more than 250 graves.

The museum is simply but sensibly laid out. The main hall, in the rear, was built over the excavation site. Two smaller exhibition halls by the entrance display unearthed items, drawings and explanatory notes in both Chinese and English.

From the implements and utensils discovered, archaeologists have learned a great deal about the daily life of Banpo. It was a typical Yangshao Culture community. Two to three hundred people lived there, practising slash-and-burn agriculture. They depended on millet and pork for their existence. In addition to millet, they planted vegetables such as cabbage and mustard, and hemp which was used to make clothing. They kept pigs, dogs and perhaps chickens and other animals. They also hunted and fished. They fired and painted extraordinarily beautiful clay pots with both abstract and non-abstract designs. The earlier decorations on these vessels portrayed fish with mouths open, fishing-nets and deer on the run—subjects reflecting the main preoccupations of Banpo's inhabitants. Gradually, as the displayed pots show quite clearly, the designs became abstract: the fish motif, for instance, was later replaced by a geometric pattern.

Chinese archaeologists believed that a primitive communist matriarchal clan lived at Banpo. In the communal burial ground found to the north of the site, men and women were buried separately, usually by themselves, sometimes in multiple single-sex graves. Examples of these graves are on display. Women were generally interred with a greater number of funeral objects than men. However, it has been pointed out by foreign archaeologists that in most early matriarchal settlements, excavated elsewhere, whole families related through the female line have been found buried together.

The Banpo Museum is located at the eastern end of the city, a convenient stop on the way to or from the Terracotta Warriors. It can be reached by bus number 11 or 42 from the Railway Station. It is open every day 9 am–5.30 pm.

REMAINS OF THE CAPITALS OF THE WESTERN ZHOU

Bronze metallurgy was practised from about the middle of the second millennium BC, contemporary with the emergence of the Shang dynasty. During this period (1600–1027 BC), the Wei and Jing valleys were dominated by a relatively backward people called the Zhou. Under their leader, King Wu, they attacked and captured Anyang, the capital of the Shang in 1027 BC. The Zhou dynasty lasted formally until 29 BC, but the kings only enjoyed real power until 771 BC. This period is called the Western Zhou. Archaeologists have discovered the remains of two Zhou palaces west of Xi'an, at Fengchu village, Qishan County, and at Zhaochen village, Fufeng County.

A Western Zhou chariot burial pit was unearthed at Zhangjiapo, Chang'an County, in 1955. The war chariot was the pre-eminent symbol of power during the Bronze Age. One of the pits excavated at Zhangjiapo contained two chariots and the remains of six horses and one slave, interred as part of the funeral of a lord. These are on display in a small museum west of the city, near Dou Men village.

It is recorded that the Zhou established five different capitals in the Wei and Jing valleys at different times. Two of these have been identified. Fengjing on the eastern bank of Feng River was an early capital. Haojing on the opposite bank was the capital from 1027 to 771 BC. The sites have been excavated and the remains of

houses, workshops, burials and some hoards of bronze articles have been found and removed to the Xianyang and Shaanxi history museums. Nothing of the old capitals can now be seen at the original sites.

Period Two: The Qin Empire

Background

THE RISE OF QIN

The Eastern Zhou began with the re-establishment of the capital near Luoyang, Henan Province, in 770 BC. The dynasty is divided into two periods, the Spring and Autumn Annals (770–476 BC) and the Warring States (475–221 BC), both taken from the names of books. During the former the Zhou kings were only nominal leaders and the Chinese world was divided into more than 100 petty principalities; by the beginning of the latter, these had been absorbed into seven much larger states.

The Warring States period was the beginning of the Iron Age in China, a time of tremendous technological progress in the arts of both war and peace. In due course Qin—based near modern Xi'an—became the most powerful of the contending states, and flourished as the result of a single-minded emphasis on military prowess, public works and food production.

THE FIRST EMPEROR

In 246 BC King Zheng came to the Qin throne, a mere boy of 13. During his reign Qin superiority was finally established when the six other states were annexed between 230 and 221 BC, unifying China for the first time.

King Zheng took the title of Qin Shihuangdi, First Emperor of Qin. (The term *huangdi* had previously only been used for deities and mythological hero-rulers such as the Yellow Emperor. Qin itself is the origin of our word 'China'). His capital was at Xianyang (see page 37), northwest of the present-day town, on the north bank of the Wei River.

An emperor of vast ambitions and achievements, Qin Shihuangdi had a profound influence on Chinese history and culture, both in his life and death. The colossal scale and careful detail of his army of terracotta warriors shows beyond any doubt the advanced state of artistic and technological development of ancient Chinese culture, which historians in China have always claimed.

The great clay army is certainly also a fitting memorial to the man who first really united what were until then disparate states. Qin Shihuangdi, who has been called both tyrant and reformer, ruled over a vast territory. Having gained predominance

(previous pages) A kneeling archer, typical of many excavated from Pit Number Two of the Museum of Terracotta Warriors. (right) A selection of heads from the terracotta warriors; each one of the thousands of statues exhibits unique features

over various ruling states, he became the sole source of power and final authority for a centralized government in Xianyang. To consolidate his huge empire, he introduced several important reforms: he personally supervised the organization of a uniform Chinese written language and prescribed 100 officially approved surnames for all his subjects. (See Special Topic on the First Emperor on page 57 for more details on his reforms.)

The First Emperor's government was severe. He administered a strict legal code, whereby a whole family would be executed for the crimes of one of its members; he taxed people and conscripted millions of labourers for both military and civil projects. To safeguard the northern frontier, the existing defensive lines along the border were rebuilt and extended to become China's Great Wall. Armies were sent as far south as today's Vietnam. Roads, irrigation schemes, palaces and above all his mausoleum all required hordes of reluctant labourers. Out of a total population of 20 million, one and a half million are thought to have been called to some form of service to the State. At the same time, independent thought was suppressed: books whose contents were considered subversive were burned, and hundreds of scholars buried alive. These oppressive policies caused suffering on a huge scale, and on Qin Shihuangdi's death revolts swiftly followed.

Sights

MUSEUM OF TERRACOTTA WARRIORS AND HORSES OF EMPEROR QIN SHI HUANG

One of the major sites of interest in China and one of the best-known, this is an archaeological find on a monumental scale. Literally an army of sculptured warriors, it is a stunning display that every visitor to China should see.

The discovery of the terracotta soldiers was like a legend come true for the villagers living in the area. For centuries they had been telling stories about the ghosts who lived underground and who were unearthed whenever they dug. Then, during a drought in the spring of 1974, some farmers decided to sink a well not far from the First Emperor's tomb. As the farmers dug, they came upon (in the words of *Newsweek*), 'the clay clones of an 8,000-man army'.

When the first figures were unearthed, it was not appreciated how many there were, but gradually the significance of the discovery was realized: the emperor had decided to take an army with him to the nether world. The larger than life-size terracotta figures were found in a vault five metres (16 feet) below the surface, one and a half kilometres (less than a mile) east of the emperor's tomb itself. In fact, the practise of burying statues with the dead began around the time of the Eastern Zhou dynasty (770–256 BC) and continued until the Song dynasty (960–1279).

Excavations are still being carried out, albeit at a painstakingly slow pace, and new discoveries are continuing to be unearthed (see below) and are likely to be so for many years to come.

The Museum of Terracotta Warriors and Horses of Emperor Qin Shi Huang, about 35 kilometres (22 miles) east of Xi'an, opened in 1979. It was declared a World Heritage site by UNESCO in 1987. The original museum, a large hangar-like building is constructed over Pit Number One, the site of the original discovery in 1974. There are two other pits, only one of which, Pit Number Three, has been fully excavated. A fourth pit was discovered, but found to be empty and archaeologists have still to agree on its purpose. It could have been intended for a main echelon of soldiers, but peasant uprisings towards the end of the Qin dynasty may have prevented the completion of this pit.

TERRACOTTA TROOPS

The terracotta soldiers are remarkably realistic pieces of sculpture. Each soldier's face has individual features, prompting speculation that they were modelled from life. They have squarish faces with broad foreheads and large, thick-lipped mouths, and they wear neat moustaches, and a number have beards. Some of them have their hair in a topknot. Expressions are generally austere, eyes focussed far ahead. It is sobering to study the rows of soldiers and to compare not just their facial features, but also their varying heights, hairstyles, even the differences in the folds of their scarves, and consider the amount of work that went into making them.

The figures stand between 1.72 and 2 metres (nearly 5 feet 8 inches and 6 feet 7 inches) tall. The body, arms and legs are hollow and were formed by looping coils of clay into a kind of tube and then beating them together whilst placing a hand inside for support. This technique has been substantiated by the discovery of fingerprints and paddle marks on broken statues. The head and hands are solid and were moulded separately and fitted to the body after firing. A thin layer of clay was applied to each head and the individual features hand-sculpted. Details of the armour were also added to the body by hand.

The statues were originally painted using pigments made from minerals mixed with a binder such as animal blood or egg white. But the colour has been almost entirely lost save for a few traces of red on tassels decorating armour and flakes of pigment on some of the faces.

Tests show that the pottery figures were fired at temperatures of between 950 and 1,050°C with a level of skill that experts today have been unable to replicate with any degree of consistency.

The soldiers are divided into infantry armed with swords and spears, archers, crossbow archers, cavalry, chariot drivers officers and generals. The wooden chariots

Archaeologists painstakingly unearth some of the terracotta warriors in Pit Number Two. Statues excavated from this pit in particular have retained a fair degree of their original paint, especially the red and pink pigments

no longer exist having decayed over the centuries, but imprints of parts of them, especially wheels, remain visible in the compacted soil and their metal fittings have been excavated. Each chariot was drawn by four pottery horses, on average 1.5 metres (4 feet 11 inches) tall by 2 metres (6 feet 7 inches) long.

The terracotta troops bear real arms, made of bronze. A huge number have been unearthed: swords, daggers, billhooks, spears, halberds, axes, crossbow triggers and arrowheads. The copper-tin alloy used was combined with 11 other elements such as nickel, magnesium, cobalt and chrome, and many weapons have emerged sharp, shiny and untarnished. The arrowheads contain a poisonous percentage of lead.

The vault housing the warriors was originally a five-metre (16-feet) deep pit with foundations of rammed earth. Three-metre (ten-feet) high walls formed chambers which were paved with bricks. Pillars lining the pits supported pine-log beams and these in turn were overlaid with thick wooden planks, covered with reed mats and finally loess clay. The terracotta soldiers, horses and chariots were arranged inside. Rut marks are still visible on some of the original slopes down which the army was wheeled. The enclosure was then permanently sealed, or at least that was the intention. It appears, however, that the troops of General Xiang Yu, who had already plundered the nearby imperial tomb, Qin Ling, opened the vault in 206 BC and set fire to the roof, which collapsed, smashing the figurines in situ and preserving them in mud and ash.

THE EXCAVATIONS
Pit Number One
This pit, the first of three that were discovered over the period May 1974 to June 1976, forms the main exhibition hall at the Qin Terracotta Army Museum complex.

It consists of 11 parallel corridors running east to west, each corridor being 210 metres (230 yards) in length. The vault covers a total area of 14,260 square metres (17,055 square yards). So far, more than 2,000 of the estimated 6,000 warriors and horses in Pit One have been unearthed. Over 1,000 soldiers have been restored to standing position, in columns four abreast, standing on the original brick floor.

The excavated soldiers face east in battle formation. Three rows, each of 70 lightly armed archers, form the vanguard. They are followed by 38 columns of more heavily armoured infantry interspersed with some 40 war chariots, of which only the pottery horses remain. A single column of spearmen face north, south and west around the edge of the pit forming a protective flank.

Visitors enter the vault through the east door and walk towards the south. At the foot of a staircase, the very spot of the original discovery back in the drought-stricken spring of 1974 is marked. Proceeding down the southern flank of the vault you cross the excavations on an elevated walkway which affords views of both the completely excavated area looking back east and the partially excavated area to the western end of the vault. The grooves across the tops of the walls separating the corridors are the marks left by the decayed wooden beams. These are even more apparent in the unexcavated areas of Pit Number Two, where the imprints of entire beams can be seen as they sagged dramatically over the centuries.

Now continuing down the northern flank of the vault you see corridors sometimes covered in protective plastic, and may occasionally catch a glimpse of a half-excavated terracotta warrior, looking as if he was drowned in a sea of brown mud. At the unexcavated western end of the pit stand many half-reconstructed soldiers. Here it is often possible to observe archaeologists as they attempt to piece together the thousands of fragments of this enormous jigsaw. As it is unearthed each piece is coded, marking where it was found and to which statue it might belong. Visitors exit the vault through a small door in the northwest corner.

Pit Number Two
This pit was discovered in 1976 after extensive test drilling, but the official excavation did not begin until March 1994. Twenty metres (22 yards) northeast of Pit Number One, Pit Two houses around 900 soldiers, including kneeling and standing archers, infantrymen and charioteers, together with some 350 chariot horses, 116 cavalry horses and the remains of 89 wooden chariots. The pit covers an

area of about 6,000 square metres (7,176 square yards) and is only partially excavated. Several more years work remains in this pit alone. It is contained in a modern building constructed over the excavation itself and allows visitors to walk around the pit and observe the ongoing excavations. The artificial lighting is subdued to help preserve the findings. These include a higher incidence of warriors with vestiges of their original colouring. On 10 September 1999, workers painstakingly scraping and brushing away the compacted earth in this pit made a very unusual discovery—a kneeling archer with traces of green paint on its face. Archaeologists are still uncertain as to its significance. The theory that this could have been a mistake by a painter seems unlikely given the meticulous care that obviously went into the preparation of each of these figures.

On the north side of the building examples of some of the warriors unearthed in this pit are on display in glass cases. A stairway leads to a second floor exhibition hall where more exhibits are to be found including just some of the more than 30,000 examples of Qin weaponry discovered in the three pits.

Pit Number Three

Discovered just one month after Pit Number Two, Pit Number Three lies 25 metres (27 yards) to the northwest of Pit Number One. It is U-shaped and at only 28.8 metres (31.5 yards) in length from east to west, 24.6 metres (27 yards) in width from north to south and covering an area of less than 500 square metres (598 square yards), Pit Number Three is by far the smallest of the three vaults. Nevertheless, archaeologists believe that, containing as it does a war chariot, 68 warriors and numerous bronze weapons, this pit represents the headquarters or command post of the garrison guarding Qin Shihuangdi in the afterlife, exercising military control over the other two larger pits of infantry.

Pit Number Three is housed within a modern building. The excavations are well labelled and atmospherically illuminated by spotlights rather than by natural light as in Pit Number One. Bilingual interpretive panels are positioned on the surrounding hand rails, and colour photographs give the visitor a useful retrospective of the excavation process, at the same time conveying something of the excitement at unearthing such a treasure trove.

The excavations lie between 5.2 and 5.4 metres (17 and 17.7 feet) below ground. Terracotta warriors, mainly headless, and the four draught horses of a chariot stand upon a fine Qin brick floor. Within the pit, rammed earth walls form chambers housing small detachments. Timbers once completed this subterranean vault structure, but these had collapsed and damaged the warriors beneath. Although many of the figures are decapitated, they compensate for their damage by exhibiting fine pigmentation.

BRONZE CHARIOTS

Housed in the exhibition hall to the left-hand side of the hangar built over the terracotta warriors are two magnificent bronze chariots.

In August 1978, as archaeologists took samples around the mausoleum of the First Emperor, they recovered a gold ornament the size of a walnut some 20 metres (22 yards) to the west of the emperor's tomb. Two years later the chariots were recovered and in the following year, 1981, the discovery was announced. Black and white pictures illustrating the progressive excavation are posted on the walls of the exhibition room. They were originally placed one behind the other facing west in a wooden coffin about 7 metres (23 feet) long and 2.3 metres (7.5 feet) wide.

The second and larger of the two chariots weighs 1,241 kilograms (2,736 pounds) and at 2.86 metres (9.38 feet) in length and 1.07 metres (3.51 feet) in height is thought to be half the actual size. The chariot therefore seems likely to have been crafted specifically for Qin Shihuangdi's afterlife, although it is thought he used such a vehicle for his inspection tours. Called *wenliangche*, the chariot for tour and inspection, this was the limousine of its day. Sliding lattice windows are set into the sides and back of the carriage for ventilation. The roof is an umbrella-like canopy symbolizing the round sky. Stylized clouds are painted on the interior ceiling and, from silk fragments discovered inside, it is thought some accessories—maybe cushions or quilts—had once made the royal passenger comfortable. This predates the more widespread use and export of silk by several centuries. In total the emperor's chariot has 3,462 separate components of gold, silver or bronze.

The first chariot may have been a vanguard chariot, running before that of the emperor. It is called *liche*, a battle chariot and, like the second, is drawn by four horses. Horsepower to weight ratio suggests that both these vehicles could have

The second and larger of the two bronze chariots on display at the Museum of Terracotta Warriors. Approximately half life size, this one was designed to carry the spirit of Qin Shihuangdi in the afterlife

The intricate detail of the liche or battle chariot clearly showing the
superb craftsmanship involved in its creation

covered ground fairly swiftly. There is no compartment in the vanguard chariot; to accommodate the standing driver the canopy is correspondingly much higher than that of the *wenliangche*—1.68 metres (5.5 feet) high—and displays superb gold decorative work on the post of the umbrella, which is locked in place by a special key. The chariot carries a pair of bronze shields, a crossbow and arrow, and a box containing 66 bronze arrowheads. The total weight of the first chariot is 1,061 kilograms (2,339 pounds) and consists of 3,064 components.

Both chariots highlight the superb metallurgical and metal-shaping technology of the Qin period, as well as its highest artistic standards. On the roof and body of the two chariots are designs of clouds, dragons and phoenixes and other various motifs. Most fittings are of solid bronze, often painted, although their pigments have faded. The harness and reins are inlaid with gold and silver, and each horse wears a halter made of some 84 one-centimetre (0.4-inch)-long tubes, fitted one onto another and thus endowed with a flexibility close to rope or leather. A tassel hangs down from each horse's neck. The canopies are incredibly thin bronze sheets but their casting is even and smooth. They are laid over a frame of 36 bow-shaped spokes about six millimetres (0.24 inches) in diameter. All these dimensions suggest to the archaeologists that both the temperature control and the casting methods were by this time highly advanced. Many parts of the chariots are overlaid with chains fashioned from extremely fine copper wire, some of the strands are only 0.5 millimetres (0.02 inches) in diameter. Microscopic examination shows that these strands were not forged but were drawn out to this size before being welded into rings and chains.

The chariot drivers and horses are also of solid bronze, yet despite their material they appear lifelike. Artisans probably used files on the figures to reproduce the appearance of hair. The horses, painted white to mimic hide and given realistically flared nostrils, convey the impression that they are ready to stride forth at the crack of the charioteer's whip.

A new museum has now been constructed to provide a better environment in which to house the bronze chariots as well as many of the other artefacts unearthed from the pits and excavations around the emperor's tomb. This building stands to the right or north as one first enters the museum complex.

360-DEGREE CINEMA

Behind Pit Number One is a 360-degree cinema. Here visitors can stand in a circular theatre and watch a dramatisation of scenes from Qin Shihuangdi's conquering of the six independent states, the construction of his mausoleum, the making of the terracotta figures and their eventual destruction by soldiers of the rebel general Xiang Yu. It may be useful to see this before entering the museum itself as it could help to give a better understanding of what is on display.

THE LATEST DISCOVERIES

In 1998, during a test excavation 150 metres to the southeast of the emperor's tomb mound, archaeologists made some further exciting discoveries. Not actually unearthed until August 1999, they include 80 pieces of stone armour. Made of grey limestone they were strung together with copper wire in a fish-scale formation similar to that sculpted on the terracotta warriors and characteristic of later Han-dynasty iron armour. The excavation also unearthed a 212 kilogram (467 pound) bronze tripod vessel or ding, and ten pottery figurines with remnants of short skirts around their torsos. It is hoped that these finds will be on display to the public before too long. Work at this and other digs is continuing and is likely to yield yet more discoveries.

QIN LING, THE MAUSOLEUM OF THE FIRST EMPEROR

Qin Shihuangdi began supervising the construction of the Qin Ling, his burial tomb, as soon as he took the throne in 246 BC. Work intensified after the conquest of the rival states, with 700,000 labourers conscripted to build it. The site chosen was south of the Wei River beside the slopes of Black Horse Mountain in what is now Lintong County, 30 kilometres (18 miles) from Xi'an. The exterior of the mausoleum is in the form of a low earth pyramid with a wide base about 350 metres (382 yards) square. Originally it was 115 metres (377 feet) high, but more than 2,000 years of erosion have reduced this to 76 metres (249 feet). Investigation by the Chinese has confirmed that there was an inner and outer enclosure. The mausoleum is thought to have been plundered at least once, by a rebel general called Xiang Yu in 206 BC, but no excavations have yet been done. The official line is that Chinese archaeologists are reluctant to open the tomb until they know a way to preserve what may be very delicate remains.

It is known, however, that not only was the body of Qin Shihuangdi interred in the tomb (in 209 BC, a year after his death), but also those of his childless wives—who were buried alive—together with artisans who had knowledge of the inner structure of the mausoleum.

Information about the construction of the mausoleum comes almost entirely from the brush of Sima Qian, the author of *The Historical Records*, China's first large-scale work of history which was written about a century after the fall of Qin.

According to Sima, heaven and earth were represented in the central chamber of the tomb. The ceiling formed the sky with pearls for stars. The floor was of a physical map of the world in stone; the 100 rivers of the empire flowed mechanically with mercury. Tests on the mausoleum have shown minute traces of mercury over an estimated area of 12,000 square metres (14,352 square yards), adding substance to this claim.

Continued on page 60

THE FIRST EMPEROR OF CHINA

Qin Shihuangdi, the First Emperor of China, was both a reformer and a tyrant. Although his reign lasted little more than a decade, it was epoch-making in terms of its enduring influence on Chinese civilization.

While the emperor is best known by most people for his amazing tomb with its terracotta guards, perhaps his most valuable legacy is a uniform Chinese script which permits people speaking different regional dialects to have a means of communication. Qin Shihuangdi standardized more than the writing of characters, however. The demands of trade required a currency with recognized fixed value throughout his vast conquered territory, so he standardized the coinage, introducing a circular copper coin with a square hole in the centre. Equally important reforms were the standardization of weights and measures, and codification of the law. A very good exhibit on Qin Shihuangdi's reforms can be found in the National Museum of Shaanxi History.

To organize the empire Qin Shihuangdi abolished the prevailing feudal system and established prefectures and counties. These were put under the administration of officials appointed by the central government. Such extensive control required roads, which Qin Shihuangdi ordered to be built, the main ones radiating from his capital, Xianyang. To protect his northern border against hostile nomads, he strengthened the pre-existing fortifications, and the line of defence now known as the Great Wall is attributed to him. It is said that he joined up stretches of frontier walls that were constructed by his predecessors to make one long barrier.

Chinese tour guides and literature promote the Great Wall as a symbol of China's ancient civilization, but in the eyes of modern Chinese it epitomizes their country's isolation and backwardness. Its construction was achieved at huge expense, particularly in terms of human lives. Labourers were conscripted to work on the wall, and

The resolute expression of a kneeling archer freshly unearthed after having lain buried for over 2,000 years. Water is used to soften the surrounding earth during excavation which accounts for the statue appearing darker than normal

Characters of an *(peace), and* ma *(horse), used by the Six Warring States*
(annexed by the Kingdom of Qin)

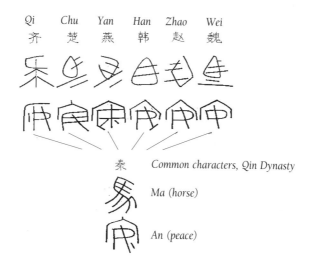

Qi	Chu	Yan	Han	Zhao	Wei
齐	楚	燕	韩	赵	魏

秦   *Common characters, Qin Dynasty*

Ma (horse)

An (peace)

Coins of the Six Warring States (annexed by the Kingdom of Qin)

Han	Chu	Wei	Yan	Qi	Zhao
韩	楚	魏	燕	齐	赵

After minting, the coins were slotted onto a wooden pole and the edges filed. Being square-holed they did not rotate.

Common currency, Qin Dynasty

秦

Characters for ban liang *(half liang). The liang was a unit of weight; 16 liang equal 1 jin. Each of these coins was 1/32nd of a jin.*

Drawn by Wang Fan (not to scale)

convicts served out sentences there. Some convict labourers even had 'perpetual' sentences, which meant that when they died their places were inherited by family members.

There are many folk tales recounting the horrors of forced labour. The legend of Meng Jiangnu is the best known. Meng Jiangnu's husband had been conscripted to work for a season on the Great Wall. When, by the end of summer, he had still not returned to his Shaanxi home, she decided to take him warm clothes for the winter. After a difficult journey she found his work gang in Hebei, but his fellow conscripts told Meng that her husband had already died. At this tragic news, Meng began to cry hysterically, and her flood of tears broke open a part of the Great Wall, revealing her husband's remains. He had been buried where he fell and his body was used as part of the fill for the wall.

On hearing of the damage to his project, an enraged Qin Shihuangdi, coincidentally present on an inspection tour, ordered Meng to be brought before him. His fury soon subsided on seeing her beauty. Although he offered to take her as concubine, she decided that death was preferable and threw herself into the Yellow Sea.

The emperor did not live long and his death in 210 BC, while away from his capital on tour, led to the fall of his dynasty shortly after. There is a story of how his Prime Minister, fearful that news of the emperor's death would spark rebellion, tried to conceal it. The emperor's body was transported in haste back to Xianyang, the Qin capital near modern Xi'an. To mask the stench of the putrefying corpse, the minister filled his chariot with rotting fish. But the feared revolt was only postponed; four years later Qin Shihuangdi's heir was killed by rebels and the Han dynasty was established soon after.

All manner of treasures were piled inside for the emperor's opulent afterlife. Crossbows were set up and positioned to shoot automatically if the interior was disturbed. After it was sealed the tomb was grassed over to appear as a natural hill. It is still like that today, although a stairway has now been built to the top, from which there is a good view of the surrounding area.

Near the mausoleum many ancillary tombs have been discovered. Some occupants were probably victims of the Second Emperor in the power struggle following the death of Qin Shihuangdi. In addition, some large graves, suspected to be those of Qin Shihuangdi's parents, have also been discovered in the area, as well as the graves of a general and of some 70 Qin labourers together with large numbers of horse skeletons. Other pits have revealed terracotta birds and animals, symbolizing the emperor's love of hunting.

So far more than 400 attendant burial pits and tombs have been discovered, covering an area of 56.25 square kilometres (nearly 22 square miles). The artefacts so far unearthed combined with historical records, indicate that Qin Shihuangdi's mausoleum was actually a miniature replica of the Qin Empire. None of the sites of these finds have so far been put on view to the public.

REMAINS OF XIANYANG

Xianyang, a satellite city of Xi'an, was established on the north bank of the Wei River in around 350 BC, when Qin was one of several warring states vying for supremacy. The city was adopted as the Qin capital, and is said to have developed into a metropolis with 800,000 inhabitants before rebel general Xiang Yu set fire to it in 206 BC.

In 1961 the exact location of the city was re-discovered in the Yaodian People's Commune northwest of Xi'an. Excavations in the 1960s and 1970s revealed the foundations of the Xianyang Palace, the First Emperor's principal domicile, partly built on a terrace of pounded earth. The structure and function of different parts of the palace are now known. Important discoveries were made, including the remains of some murals. Building materials, decorated bricks and tiles were found in large quantities. These remains, other artifacts from the period, and a wooden model of the palace, can be seen in the Xianyang Museum.

Most visitors, however, go to the museum to view its collection of miniature terracotta soldiers dating from the Han dynasty (see page 68). The museum itself is housed in an attractive collection of buildings that originally functioned as a Confucius temple and was constructed during the Ming dynasty in 1371. Apart from the Qin artifacts and Han figurines, the museum also has a small display of steles and Buddhist statues and stonework (part of the museum now functions as a Buddhist temple). The museum is on Zhongshan Jie which is a continuation of Xining Jie.

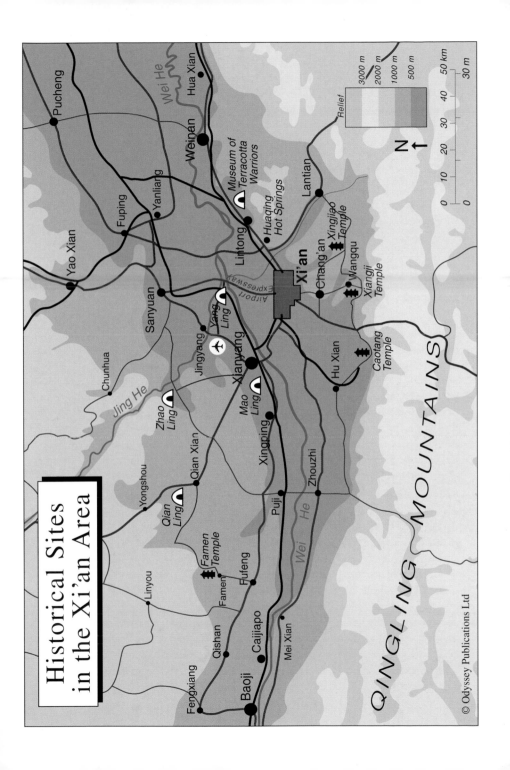

Historical Sites in the Xi'an Area

© Odyssey Publications Ltd

Xianyang is now Shaanxi's booming third city and site of the airport serving Xi'an, 28 kilometres (17 miles) away. It is accessible from Xi'an by road or rail. Mini buses depart frequently from the bus station near the southwest corner of the city wall. The ride takes about one hour.

REMAINS OF AFANG PALACE

In 212 BC the First Emperor decided to build a new and larger principal palace on the other side of the Wei River, some 10 kilometres (6 miles) west of Xi'an. Afang Palace was never finished, but the raised platform of pounded earth remains to this day.

Period Three: The Han Dynasty

Background

The Qin dynasty maintained its authority only until 209 BC. The First Emperor's death in 210 BC was followed by outbreaks of rebellion and civil war, which led to the empire's dissolution. The final blow was dealt by General Xiang Yu, who conquered the Qin forces in 207 BC. But then he himself was overthrown four years later by the founder of the Han dynasty.

The first Han emperor was a general of plebeian background called Liu Bang, known posthumously by his dynastic title of Han Gaozu, which literally means great-great-grandfather of Han. His capital, called Chang'an, was built in the strategic Wei valley. Accordingly the first half of Han rule, lasting until AD 8, is called the Western Han to distinguish it from the Eastern Han period, AD 25–220, when the capital was at Luoyang to the east.

THE CAPITAL CITY OF CHANG'AN

In 202 BC Liu Bang moved into a minor Qin palace on the southern side of the Wei. Later the architect Xiao He added a large new complex of some 40 buildings to the west of it. This was the Weiyang Palace (see page 67), which was to remain the principal seat of the Western Han emperors. Together these two palaces formed the nucleus of Han-dynasty Chang'an.

The imperial establishment soon outgrew the two original palaces and more buildings were added during the time of the emperor Han Huidi (reigned 194–187 BC). An irregular-shaped wall was built around the palaces, eventually forming a circumference of about 22 kilometres (nearly 14 miles). Within the wall there were eight main streets and 160 alleys. Outside the wall another city developed, a city of artisans, with markets, workshops and houses.

THE SILK ROAD

It was during the Han that the Chinese opened up routes to central and western Asia. This was to have a profound impact on Chang'an.

From the capital, Han Wudi, the Martial Emperor (reigned 140–86 BC), launched a series of campaigns against the Xiongnu, the warlike Turkish people of the steppes, who were a constant threat to the northern frontier of China. In 139 BC Zhang Qian was sent officially to central Asia to find allies against the Xiongnu. On his second journey in 119 BC he went as far as the Ili Valley, on the present-day border with the CIS and from there dispatched envoys to India and the Iranian Empire as well as kingdoms east of the Caspian Sea. One of the most influential finds that Zhang Qian made on this journey were the splendid horses in what is now Uzbekistan. Some of these were brought to China where they later became the inspiration of Chinese sculptors, painters and writers to an extent that was almost obsessional, especially during the Tang dynasty.

Merchant caravans followed the armies and established the routes of what Europeans later called the Silk Road. The eastern section opened by the Chinese linked with trade routes in western Asia to form links of trade and cultural exchange stretching from Chang'an to the ports of the eastern Mediterranean Sea. Official contact with the Roman Empire was attempted in AD 97, but the envoy never got through. However, unofficial representatives of Rome, including a party of jugglers, reportedly arrived in Chang'an in AD 120. There was a special street where foreigners were accommodated, and even a protocol department to arrange their reception.

Paper was one of many Chinese inventions that eventually reached Europe via the Silk Road. The world's earliest pieces of paper were discovered in 1957 at Ba Bridge, east of Xi'an. It was originally thought that paper was invented during the Eastern Han, but these pieces of hemp paper were made considerably earlier, during the reign of Han Wudi.

THE IMPERIAL TOMBS OF THE WESTERN HAN DYNASTY

There are nine tombs of the Western Han emperors on the north bank of the Wei River and two south of the present city of Xi'an. The construction of each one was started soon after the accession of the sovereign and, according to regulations, one third of all state revenues was devoted to the project. On the death of the emperor valuable objects were placed in the tomb and the body was interred in a suit of jade plates, sewn together with gold wire. A piece of jade was placed in the mouth of the emperor. Prominent members of the imperial family and important officials were buried in smaller ancillary or satellite tombs nearby.

None of the imperial mausoleums has been excavated, and they remain irregular flat-topped grassy pyramids, 33–46 metres (108–151 feet) high.

Sights

MAO LING, THE MAUSOLEUM OF EMPEROR HAN WUDI

Mao Ling is the tomb of Han Wudi, the Martial Emperor, who came to the throne in 140 BC, ruling for 54 years. Like Qin Shihuangdi, he initiated a new period of dynamic expansion. Imperial rule was extended to the southeast coastal region of China, northern Vietnam and northern Korea. His tomb is 40 kilometres (25 miles) west of Xi'an. Although it has not been excavated, the commemorative area has been well laid out. The top of the small hill on which a monument has been built has a good view of many surrounding tombs, some of which have been excavated.

The Martial Emperor had tried to avoid his burial with attempts at making himself immortal. He put a bronze statue (the Brazen Immortal) in a high tower to catch the pure dew in a bowl, which he drank with powdered jade. However, the potion proved ineffective, and he died in his 70th year. Apparently there were so many treasures intended for his tomb that they could not all be fitted in. But many of his books are said to have been buried with him, as well as a number of live animals.

The mausoleum was desecrated, rather than robbed, by peasant rebels called the Red Eyebrows, just before the establishment of the Eastern Han. They removed articles from the tomb and threw them on a bonfire. Archaeologists believe that they have found the patch of burnt earth where this happened.

Mao Ling is situated northwest of Xi'an, a convenient stop on the way to or from Qian Ling, the Tang-dynasty tombs (see page 78).

THE TOMB OF HUO QUBING

About one and a half kilometres (less than a mile) from the mausoleum of the Martial Emperor is the even more interesting tomb of his eminent general. Nicknamed the 'Swift Cavalry General', Huo Qubing, later Grand Marshal, was born in 140 BC. His uncle took him to fight the fierce northern nomads, the Xiongnu, when he was 18. He led a force of 800 cavalry which is reputed to have killed more than 2,000 of the enemy. In all he defeated the Xiongnu in six battles and kept open the transportation route between Xi'an and the northwestern province of Gansu. He died at the age of only 24 from natural causes. According to the author Sima Qian, who was a contemporary, the Martial Emperor built a special tomb for the general in the shape of the Qilian Mountain (which marks the present-day border of Gansu and Qinghai provinces), where Huo had won a great victory.

The tomb has been almost certainly identified by the discovery of 16 remarkable stone sculptures. All are at the site. In front of the tomb mound, are two horses, each in a pavilion. One of them is galloping and the other apparently trampling a

(preceding pages) The naked figurines from Yang Ling the mausoleum of Jingdi the fourth emperor of the Han dynasty. The remains of iron swords lie beside some of them, but their once movable wooden arms and real clothes have long since decayed.

Xiongnu. The other sculptures are laid out in two covered corridors on either side of the mound. They include various animals including a tiger, boar, elephant and ox, a toad and frog, and two strange human figures, perhaps demons or gods, one of which is wrestling with a bear. This last stone, about 2.77 metres (nine feet) high, may represent a Xiongnu idol. Huo Qubing brought back at least one of these, known as the 'Golden Man'.

The two halls that serve as a museum are either side of an attractively laid out garden complete with goldfish pond. The exhibits inside are almost all of the Western Han period and were discovered in the area of the Mao Ling.

Perhaps the star exhibit is a magnificent rhinoceros, the body of which is decorated with a cloud design inlaid with gold and silver. It is in fact a zun, or wine vessel. Also on display is an attractive gold and silver plated bamboo-shaped censer with dragon decoration and a gilded horse. Given the rather insecure nature of these buildings, these items are reproductions, the originals being safely stored in the Shaanxi History Museum. There are also a number of bronze articles, including money, agricultural implements, and examples of the decorated building materials for which both the Qin and Han were famous. An interesting pictorial map is also on display showing the layout of the Han tombs in the Xi'an area.

REMAINS OF THE HAN CITY OF CHANG'AN

HAN CITY WALLS

The site of the Han capital is on the northwestern edge of the present-day city of Xi'an. Today the walls are still there but inside the palaces have been replaced by fields of wheat and rape-seed.

REMAINS OF WEIYANG PALACE

The southern part of the Han city was excavated between 1957 and 1959 so the layout of the palaces is known. The raised area of the audience hall of Weiyang Palace, the principal seat of the Western Han emperors, can be reached by road. The platform is 101 metres (330 feet) long, much smaller than was thought for the original hall, but we know that the Weiyang was rebuilt several times during the Tang period, so it is likely that the foundations have been altered.

HAN CITY ARMOURY

Built in 200 BC, the armoury occupied 23 hectares (57 acres) near the present-day village of Daliuzhai, next to the site of Weiyang Palace. Excavations have revealed a large number of iron weapons, and some made of bronze. At the end of 1981 it was announced that a number of hefty suits of armour had been found weighing 35–40 kilograms (77–88 pounds).

HAN TERRACOTTA ARMY

The prime exhibit in the Xianyang Museum (see page 60) is a superb collection of 3,000 miniature terracotta warriors. They were found in 1965 in two of a group of Han tombs known as Yangjiawan Tombs near the village of the same name 20 kilometres (12 miles) to the east of Xianyang. They were in the area of the tomb of Han Gaozu who, as Liu Bang, founded the Han dynasty in 206 BC, and were probably part of a tomb of a high-ranking military official of the early Han period.

The terracotta infantrymen and cavalrymen, about 35 and 50 centimetres (13.8 and 19.7 inches) in height respectively, were found in battle formation in two rows of five rectangular pits, to the east and west, with a pit containing war chariots in the centre. (The chariots were originally constructed of pottery and wood. The wood had decayed and the pottery remains were broken into so many pieces it was unfortunately impossible to reconstruct them.)

The army is displayed in two halls in the formation in which they were discovered. At first the soldiers look identical, but on closer examination several subtle differences can be seen. There are photographs on the wall with captions in Chinese and English, that clearly explain the difference. There are in fact three distinct ethnic types amongst the statues: the Cong people from Sichuan Province, the Longxi from Gansu and the Guanzhong from Shaanxi.

The eastern pits contain mostly infantrymen. Their empty hands once held wooden weapons and pottery shields, the latter are on display in the cabinets. The figurines were originally painted and some show traces of colour, although the paint on a few is well-preserved.

The cavalry are concentrated in the western pits and are of two distinct kinds: taller, heavy-uniformed cavalrymen, some in armour, riding larger and stronger horses, and relatively shorter men with light uniforms riding smaller horses. The latter are archers and wear quivers on their backs.

Like a massive army posed for battle the warriors are an impressive sight making the ride from Xi'an well worthwhile.

YANG LING

Next to the road leading from Xi'an to the new airport near Xianyang, just across the bridge spanning the Wei River, is an archaeological site that has the potential to eclipse even that of the Terracotta Army. On the south side of the road stands a brand new museum; officially opened to the public at the end of September 1999, it houses just some of the remarkable findings so far unearthed during the ten years since the site was first discovered.

Yang Ling or Han Yang Mausoleum is the site of the tomb of Liu Qi the fourth Han emperor Jingdi (reigned 157 BC–141 BC). His tomb mound stands on the north side of the road opposite the museum, together with that of his wife who died some 15 years later. To date archaeologists have concentrated on excavating pits in the immediate surrounding area and, as with the mausoleum of Qin Shihuangdi, they have left the emperor's tomb untouched for the time being.

Work began on the site with the excavation of 24 pits to the south of the road containing the emperor's army. The remains of several hundred thousand pottery warriors were unearthed. Their bodies are approximately one third life-size, without arms and naked, but with traces of red silk present on some of them. Their arms were originally made of wood, but these, together with the leather armour they once wore, have long since decayed. Whereas the Han terracotta army figurines in the Xianyang Museum display facial characteristics of three ethnic groups, the warriors of Yang Ling are of at least ten different ethnic variations.

Archaeologists later turned their attention to the pits surrounding the tombs themselves. The emperor's tomb mound was originally square-sided with a flat top, in the shape of a truncated pyramid 31 metres (102 feet) high, and was contained within a square walled enclosure, each side of which was 410 metres (448 yards) long with a gate in the middle. Four brick culverts that acted as drains for the tomb have been unearthed, one at each of the four corners. A road led from each gate with a rammed-earth tower standing on either side. More than 90 pits have been discovered arranged in parallel rows running perpendicular to the four sides of the

(opposite and above) Heads of the figurines excavated at Yang Ling exhibit facial characteristics of at least ten different ethnic variations. Many retain much of their original paintwork including the skin colour and black-painted hair, pupils and moustaches.

tomb. A further 28 pits have been found around the tomb of the emperor's consort, Empress Wang, who died 15 years after Jingdi in 126 BC. Excavation of these pits is still continuing, but so far they have revealed some 40,000 pottery figurines and over 2,000 pottery animals.

The figurines include soldiers, male and female archers mounted on horseback, servants, both standing and kneeling, musicians and dancers. The latter, in particular, display a superb grace with lithe bodies and flowing, long sleeved dresses. All the figurines were painted and many still retain at least their original basic ochre colouring representing the skin. Features such as the hair, eyebrows, moustache, and pupils were painted in black. There are patches of bright vermillion around the heads of some with traces of woven silk fabric, apparently the remains of a kind of a kind of headband worn during this peroid. Similar traces around the shins show that some wore red silk leggings. Some servant figurines have been unearthed in almost perfect condition. These, like the dancers, were moulded wearing clothes, in this case with white painted robes and yellow belts.

The domesticated animals include horses, cows, pigs (some of which are clearly pregnant), sheep, goats, dogs and chickens. The horses have a slot along the back of the neck where a mane was once fixed and a hole for a tail, but these have decayed, perhaps originally made from real horse's hair.

It would appear that each pit represents a division or department of the emperor's palace. In fact some of the pits have revealed rooms complete with servants and everyday utensils. The inclusion of domestic animals is of particular interest to archaeologists as this is the first time such a quantity and variety has been discovered. Following the unification and standardisation of the Qin dynasty, the Chinese under the Han emperors experienced a relatively stable and prosperous period with the rapid development of agriculture. The finds at Yang Ling represent a miniature of daily life at the Han palace of Chang'an.

It has been estimated that around 17,000 workers, housed in the nearby city of Yang Ling to the east, took 28 years to complete work on the main tombs and their associated pits.

A team of about 30 archaeologists, students and assistants are currently employed at the site, where initial testing of the ground must be carried out by hand. As with all such sites, the archaeologist must first use a long metal rod to take core samples from the ground around the tombs. By studying the colour of the soil samples, experience can tell whether the earth has at one time been disturbed and so indicate the possible site of a pit. It is only in this laborious way that a picture can be built up of the layout of an archaeological site before the actual digging can begin.

The Shaanxi provincial government have given significant funding to develop this project and to ensure its preservation. The site was visited by President Jiang

Zemin in June 1999. It is very highly recommended and due to its convenient location beside the airport road can easily be included on any itinerary.

Period Four: The Tang Dynasty

Background

The collapse of the Han dynasty in AD 220 after years of insoluble economic and political problems was followed by centuries of power struggles, barbarian invasions and political fragmentation, with interludes of unity and order. In AD 581 a high ranking official, Yang Qian, seized the throne and founded the Sui dynasty.

THE SUI AND THE CAPITAL CITY OF DAXINGCHENG

The old Han city of Chang'an was by then too derelict to serve as the symbol of power for the first Sui emperor, who reigned with the title of Wendi. He commissioned a brilliant engineer, Yuwen Kai, to build a new city—Daxingcheng, or the City of Great Revival—southeast of the old one.

Yang Qian and Yuwen Kai created perhaps one of the greatest planned cities. The huge rectangular area designated for the metropolis faced the four cardinal points and had an outer wall with a perimeter of over 36 kilometres (22 miles).

The Sui dynasty was, however, short lived. Wendi was succeeded by his even more ambitious son, the emperor Sui Yangdi. He, in turn, ordered the construction of a new capital at Luoyang, as well as a huge programme of canal building (the Grand Canal, the world's largest man-made waterway running from Luoyang to Hangzhou, was his most monumental legacy to China). He also attempted a disastrous invasion of Korea. Rebellions followed and the emperor was assassinated in Yangzhou in AD 618.

THE ESTABLISHMENT OF THE TANG DYNASTY

Power was next seized by the Li family. Li Yuan, hereditary Duke of Tang, marched on Daxingcheng in AD 617 and the following year made himself emperor with the title of Tang Gaozu. The capital was renamed Chang'an, a deliberate move to assume by implication the mantle of the Han. In turn, Tang Gaozu was ousted by his second son, Li Shimin, who took the throne himself with the title of Tang Taizong, and effectively consolidated the Tang.

The Tang dynasty is widely considered to be a Golden Age, the stage in history when Chinese civilization reached its most glorious and sophisticated. The Tang empire was the largest, richest, most sophisticated state in the world. And Chang'an

(Xi'an) was again the centre and symbol of this glory, the world's largest and most splendid city. Only the Baghdad of Harun al Rashid offered any comparison. During this period, the city wall of Chang'an stretched far beyond the one standing today, which was built during the later Ming period, and went as far as the Big Goose Pagoda. By the middle of the eighth century China had a population estimated at 53 million, of which nearly two million lived in the capital.

EMPRESS WU

Taizong died in AD 649 and was succeeded by his ninth son, who reigned with the title of Gaozong until 683. However, the next effective ruler was a woman, not a man. Wu Zetian (see page 89) was born in AD 624 and became a concubine of Taizong. On his death she withdrew from court and became a Buddhist nun, only to be recalled by Gaozong, eventually becoming his empress in AD 655.

After Gaozong's death Wu Zetian dethroned two of her sons and her official reign began in AD 690. Although Empress Wu's rule was characterized by recurrent palace intrigues and ruthless political murders, China prospered greatly during this time.

For economic as well as political reasons she preferred Luoyang to Chang'an and chose this as her capital from AD 683 to 701. Just before her death in AD 705, when she was in her 80s, she was finally removed from power, and the Tang re-established.

THE REIGN OF EMPEROR TANG XUANZONG

The period of struggle over the Tang succession was ended by the emergence of the third great ruler of the dynasty, Emperor Xuanzong, Empress Wu's grandson. Popularly known as Ming Huang, the

Traces of silk fabric clearly visible on the head of this figurine indicate it once wore some form of headdress. The vermillion patches are the remains of a kind of headband worn during this period

Enlightened Emperor, his reign corresponds with what is called the High Tang, the apogee of the Tang dynasty, that most confident and cosmopolitan of all phases of Chinese civilization.

The emperor presided over a brilliant, extravagant court, patronizing the greatest concentration of literary and artistic genius in Chinese history. Xuanzong's contemporaries included the paramount poets of China, Du Fu (AD 712–770) and Li Bai (AD 699–762), and the great painter Wu Daozi (AD 700–760).

After the death of his beloved Imperial Concubine Yang Guifei (see page 86), Xuanzong died a broken man in AD 762, having earlier abdicated in favour of his third son.

CHANG'AN IN THE EIGHTH CENTURY

Chang'an in the eighty century was a lively, crowded, beautiful city. Appropriate, as the planned capital of a well-ordered society, it was also highly organized.

In the centre was the Imperial City with the Imperial Secretariat, the Imperial Chancellery, the Censorate and the Department of State Affairs under which came the six Boards of Personnel, Revenue, Rites, War, Justice and Public Works. This organization of government lasted, in this form at least, for the next thousand years.

The central north-south avenue, with the delightful name of 'The Street of the Vermilion Bird', divided the Outer City into two districts: the area of the aristocrats to the east, and the rather more populated section of the merchants and lower classes to the west. The two markets which served them were very large and extremely well run. We know that the shops and workshops of the East Market were divided into 220 trades, each one with its own exclusive area and bazaar.

A pregnant pig—one of thousands of pottery animals, including horses, cattle, sheep, goats, dogs and chickens, unearthed at Yang Ling

Much of the colour in Chang'an was provided by the 'Westerners'—merchants from central Asia and Arabia, and particularly travellers from Persia.

Central Asian fashions dominated the capital. Women dressed in the Persian style and wore exotic Western jewellery. Men played polo. The Buddhist temples and monasteries vied with each other in offering unusual religious entertainment.

Foreigners congregated in the West Market, which was always full of excitement and activity. Here were bazaars and artisans' workshops, merchants' houses and hostelries, taverns and entertainment places, including wine shops where the songs and dances of central Asia were performed. There were Persian bazaars; shops of the unpopular Uygar moneylenders; and markets selling precious jewels and pearls, spices, medicinal herbs, silk, and a whole range of everyday items, including the newly fashionable beverage, tea. This was where criminals were punished and where courtesans could be found. Many of these ladies were from the lands bordering Persia and some were reputedly even blonde and blue-eyed.

FOREIGN RELIGIONS IN CHANG'AN

For much of the Tang the authorities allowed the foreign communities freedom of religion. Zoroastrianism, Manichaeism, Nestorianism and finally Islam all followed Buddhism to Chang'an (see page 94).

If you are interested in tracing the development of these religions, Xi'an's Forest of Steles Museum (see page 117) provides some intriguing evidence. Here you can see a tomb stone, dated AD 874, inscribed in Chinese and Persian Pahlavi script, originally marking the grave of Ma, wife of Suren, a Zoroastrian. Also at the museum is the celebrated Nestorian Stele. Inscriptions on this stone, in Chinese and Syriac, recorded the establishment of Chang'an's second Nestorian Christian chapel in 781.

Even the Manichees, who believed in a combination of Gnostic Christianity and Zoroastrianism, had a place of worship in Chang'an in the eighth century.

THE INFLUENCE OF CHANG'AN

If Chang'an itself was cosmopolitan, it also had unparalleled influence throughout central and eastern Asia. The royal progeny of several Korean and central Asian states, as well as Tibet, were educated in the schools and monasteries of the Tang capital. But by far the greatest transfer of Tang culture was to Japan. From the mid-seventh century to the end of the ninth century a whole series of official missions were sent by sea to China. The Japanese cities of Nara and Kyoto were built on the same plan as Chang'an, though naturally smaller. The regular layout of Kyoto still remains today, and the best examples of Tang wooden architecture also survive in Japan rather than in China.

THE DESTRUCTION OF CHANG'AN

In the ninth century the importance of Chang'an waned, with the Tang dynasty itself coming under pressure as factions jostled for power. Twice Chang'an was sacked by peasant rebels and troops of the imperial forces. In AD 904 the Tang court was moved to Luoyang. The main surviving buildings were dismantled and the beams were taken to the Wei River where they were lashed together to form rafts which were floated down to the new capital. From AD 904–906 the city walls were demolished and a new, more modest wall was built around the old Imperial City. In AD 907 the last Tang emperor was finally deposed and Chang'an was renamed Da'anfu.

THE IMPERIAL TOMBS OF THE TANG DYNASTY

From the tomb of the Emperor Xuanzong in the east to the tomb of Gaozong and Empress Wu in the west, the 18 Tang tombs are spread out in a line 120 kilometres (75 miles) long. Most of them are set into natural hills and mountains, rather than underneath artificial mounds.

Each tomb was originally surrounded by a square wall and had a series of buildings for ceremonial purposes and for the use of guards. Each had its own 'Spirit Way', an avenue lined with stone sculptures. The Tang conception was much grander than that of the Ming, as all 13 of the well-known Ming Tombs in Beijing share a common approach.

The underground palaces of the emperors remain untouched. Only the important subsidiary tombs of the Zhao Ling and Qian Ling have been excavated.

Sights

HUAQING HOT SPRINGS

A must for every visitor to Xi'an, Huaqing Hot Springs has been a favourite spa since the Tang dynasty. For centuries emperors had come here to bathe and enjoy the scenic beauty. The more energetic visitors may climb some or all of Li Mountain, on which are situated several Daoist and Buddhist temples. A cable car has now been installed to make this possible for everyone. None of the buildings in the grounds are particularly important. Although many of them are named after Tang halls and pavilions, they were built either at the end of the last century or during this one.

Huaqing Hot Springs can be conveniently visited on returning from the Terracotta Army site. A principal pleasure spot for Chinese tourists, the place is often busy, especially on Sundays.

The resort dates back to the Western Zhou when construction began on a series of pleasure resort palaces at the hot springs site, which is 30 kilometres

(18 miles) from Xi'an, at the foot of Black Horse Mountain. The First Emperor of Qin had a residence there, as did Han Wudi, the Martial Emperor. In more recent times even Chiang Kai-shek used some of the buildings. However, the strongest associations are with the Tang: Black Horse Mountain is still covered with the pine and cypress trees planted by Tang Xuanzong, and the present buildings have a Tang atmosphere.

Taizong commissioned his architect Yan Lide to design a palace, the Tangquan, in AD 644. It became the favourite resort of Xuanzong who spent every winter there from AD 745 to 755 in the company of Yang Guifei, the Imperial Concubine (see page 86). The resort was greatly enlarged in AD 747 and renamed Huaqing Palace. The complex was destroyed at the end of the Tang.

However, imperial bathing pools from this period (AD 618–907), lost for almost a millennium, were discovered in 1982 by workmen renovating the Guifei Pavilion. They uncovered remains of palace architecture, including lotus-shaped roof tile-ends and four bathing pools—the Star, Long, Lotus and Guifei pools. The Guifei or Hibiscus Pool, dating from AD 712–756, has now been restored and is open to the public—but for viewing, not for bathing. It is a terraced structure with a central, empty, pool in the shape of a Chinese crab-apple blossom. The fountainhead, designed to represent the stamens of a flower, is a reproduction of the original.

The Marble Boat and Nine Dragon Pool at Huaqing Hot Springs

THE BATHS

The best way to appreciate the Huaqing Hot Springs is, of course, to take a bath. The water rises at a constant temperature of 43°C (109°F) and contains various minerals, including lime and manganese carbonate.

The baths are exotically named. The Lotus, the Crab Apple and the Emperor's Nine Dragon Bath, for example, can be hired by the hour. Communal baths are a bargain if one does not mind mingling with 49 other bathers of the same sex. There are hot spring baths available at the Huaqing Guesthouse (see page 149) but they are reserved for guests.

THE SITE OF THE XI'AN INCIDENT

The Five Chamber Building, just behind the Imperial Concubine's Bath, contains the bedroom used by Chiang Kai-shek on the eve of the Xi'an Incident of 1936— also known as the Double Twelfth Incident as it happed on 12th December (see page 130). As the rebellious troops of Zhang Xueliang showered the pavilion with gunfire, Chiang escaped through a window and over the back wall. The broken panes of the windows can still be seen. Chiang was captured many hours later on Li Mountain. His hiding place is now marked by an iron chain. The pavilion commemorating his capture was originally erected by the Nationalists to celebrate their leader's escape.

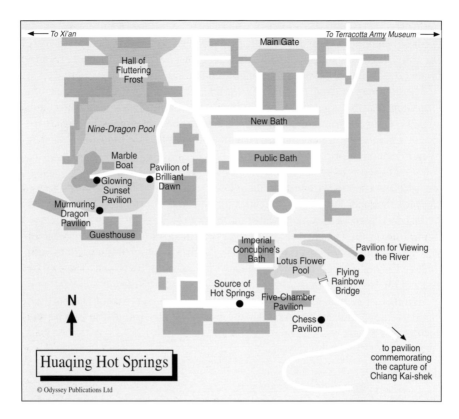

To Xi'an ←   → To Terracotta Army Museum

Main Gate

Hall of Fluttering Frost

Nine-Dragon Pool

New Bath

Marble Boat

Public Bath

Pavilion of Brilliant Dawn

Glowing Sunset Pavilion

Murmuring Dragon Pavilion

Guesthouse

Imperial Concubine's Bath

Pavilion for Viewing the River

Lotus Flower Pool

Flying Rainbow Bridge

Source of Hot Springs

Five-Chamber Pavilion

N

Chess Pavilion

Huaqing Hot Springs

to pavilion commemorating the capture of Chiang Kai-shek

© Odyssey Publications Ltd

QIAN LING

Of all the imperial tomb complexes near Xi'an Qian Ling is probably the best preserved and the most complete. It is the mausoleum of Emperor Tang Gaozong and Empress Wu Zetian (see page 89) and is situated 85 kilometres (53 miles) west of Xi'an. It has never been robbed or excavated but there are interesting relics in its vicinity.

If you stand at the southern approach to the mausoleum you can appreciate the original Tang layout and design. This main southern approach is between two prominent small hills, surmounted by reconstructed towers. From a distance the hills are said to resemble a pair of woman's breasts, and the story goes that Emperor Tang Gaozong had them constructed to honour the natural beauty of his wife.

This grand and imposing avenue of animal and human statues leading all the way to the tombs is perhaps Qian Ling's most impressive feature, creating a memorable and awe-inspiring effect. Nowadays, visitors usually arrive via the car park part way along the route. It is well worth taking the time to stroll to the southern end of the Spirit Way to fully appreciate the grandiose nature of the project. Standing at the top of the flight of steps that disappears out of view below, one has a tremendous view over the countryside to the south—if the weather is clear.

At the head of the avenue are two obelisk-like Cloud Pillars followed by a series of pairs of stone statues lining the Spirit Way to the mausoleum. First there are two winged horses, then two vermilion birds like ostriches. Five pairs of saddled horses come next, originally each had a groom but now two are missing. These are followed by ten pairs of tall, almost hieratic guardians. They have very large heads, wear long sleeved robes, and hold the hilts of long swords that rest on the ground between their feet.

Beyond the guardians are two stone memorials; the one on the left (west) commemorates the reign of Tang Gaozong and is balanced on the east side by the so called Blank Tablet in honour of Empress Wu. The original implication was apparently that the old empress was beyond praise, but memorials were in fact inscribed on it during the Song and Jin dynasties (960–1234).

North of two small earthen remains—the ruins of two watch-towers—is a remarkable collection of 61 stone figures, now headless. From the inscriptions on the backs of these figures it appears that they represent actual foreigners who came to the Chinese court in the seventh century; some were envoys of central Asian countries, others were barbarian chiefs. Behind them are two powerful sculptures of stone lions, guarding the southern entrance to the original inner enclosure, now no longer extant. There are similar pairs of animals at the north, east and west entrances. Just inside the old southern entrance is an 18th-century stele.

THE QIAN LING SATELLITE TOMBS

To the southeast of the principal mausoleum are 17 satellite tombs beneath man-made mounds. The names of the occupants are all known. Five of the tombs were excavated between 1960 and 1972. They had previously been robbed, but evidently of only gold, silver and precious gems. Archaeologists found a large number of pieces of pottery. But by far the most exciting discoveries at the sites were the mural paintings in the interiors. These provide valuable information about Tang court life, and are exquisite examples of the quality of the period's art.

Unfortunately the paintings started to deteriorate soon after the tombs had been opened. All the principal ones have now been taken to the Shaanxi History Museum, where they are kept in a special climate-controlled environment and only accessible by special arrangement. They have been replaced with reproductions, which are fairly accurate copies of the originals.

THE TOMB OF PRINCESS YONGTAI

This was the first tomb to be excavated and remains the most impressive of all the tombs that can be seen. Princess Yongtai was a granddaughter of Emperor Gaozong and Empress Wu. She died in AD 701 at the age of 17.

The circumstances surrounding her death were mysterious. According to the records she was executed by her ruthless grandmother on suspicion of having criticized some court favourites. Five years after her death her remains were exhumed and her tomb built in the Qian Ling complex. The memorial tablet inside the tomb states she died in childbirth, perhaps because the manner of her actual death was considered shameful.

When the tomb was excavated, between 1960 and 1962, archaeologists came across an unexpected and gruesome discovery: the skeleton of a tomb robber, evidently murdered by his accomplices. The modern Japanese writer Yasushi Inoue has written a short story, *Princess Yung-tai's Necklace*, based on the incident (see page 82). Although the tomb had been plundered, archaeologists still found over 1,300 artifacts, including many fine examples of tri-glazed pottery.

The passage leading down to the tomb is very steep—take care, as there are no steps. The walls on either side are decorated by reproductions of the original murals. They represent court attendants, almost all of them women, wearing the elegant central Asian fashions of the day. Set into the walls are deep alcoves containing reproductions of the tri-glazed figurines, some standing, others on horseback, and everyday utensils that were originally buried with the princess.

Towards the bottom of the passage are two large, square tombstones, the first of which is inscribed with large, ancient seal script character; the two representing Yongtai are at the top of the centre column. Nearby is the hole in the roof of the passage used by the tomb robbers.

Ducking through the heavy stone doorway, one enters the crypt with its huge sarcophagus made of black jade-stone. Called *mo yu shi* in Chinese, this stone is the same used to make the door and tombstones, and was quarried in Fuping County about 60 kilometres (37 miles) northeast of Xi'an. The sarcophagus is beautifully engraved with maidservants, phoenixes, mandarin ducks, vines and flowers and has a top carved in the form of a tiled roof. It originally contained the bodies of both the princess and her husband, Wu Yanji, who was the son of a nephew of Empress Wu and is said to have been also killed in the same year. Their remains are preserved for research in the Xi'an Medical College.

The small museum next to the tomb entrance displays a reproduction of the stone sarcophagus with part of one side removed to show the carvings both inside and out. There are also some of the original tomb figurines, reproduction frescoes and rubbings from this and other Qian Ling tombs. Continued on page 90

A reproduction of one of the murals originally decorating the tomb of Princess Yongtai, showing maidservants wearing the elegant fashions and hairstyles typical of the Tang dynasty

BETRAYAL

*T*hree nights were required to open a shaft. Most commonly the main funeral passage lay directly below the earthen mound, and the crypt itself, containing the sarcophagus, lay at some remove. Sometimes, to confuse robbers, the main passage, the inner passage, and the crypt itself bore no relation at all to the external mound. The several cuts would wind and twist, and then the door to the crypt would be at the spot least expected. Sometimes it was by no means easy even to find the crypt. Incomparably more difficult was the task of getting the funeral treasures out. These were of course the tombs of the rich and noble. They had been devised on the assumption that there would be robbers...

For three nights the ten of them took turns at digging. Some forty feet below the spot chosen by Ko they came upon a flat rock about a yard square which might have been called the skylight. The stone was too large for two or three men to move. Since they were confined to the narrow shaft they had opened, they were two nights making their way into the passage below. When finally they had succeeded, there was still a little time before daybreak. Some in the band wanted to proceed immediately, but Ch'en said with some firmness that they would wait until the next night. Against possible discovery, they had yet to block the shaft and cover it with weeds. The secret of grave robbing was to leave time for everything.

It was a cloudy night of fierce winds when they finally made their way inside. The band seemed to gather from nowhere, work clothes beating in the wind. The season was neither warm nor cold. The light of the lanterns was now bright, now low.

Ch'en looked from one to another. They were not to have thoughts of private booty, he said, they were to share alike. And he approached a young woman, the only woman among them, and a tall young man.

'You two will stand guard outside,' he said.

The woman was his third wife, the man his younger brother.

'Get inside, the rest of you.'

As if in a sort of ceremonial capacity as leader, he took up a lantern and bent over to enter the dark hold. Three men followed him and mattocks and shovels and hammers and the like were brought down, and the other four disappeared inside.

The darkness was more profound than on the surface. The only sound was the whistling of the wind. He had left as sentinels his wife and a brother with whom he shared the same blood, and in the choice had been considerations of a sort that Ch'en would make. Had he chosen anyone else, he could not have been sure when the stone would be toppled back into place. The others were his trusted comrades, but they were human, and he could not be sure when temptation would raise its head. If the stone were to fall, if only that were to happen, then the men inside would not see the light of day again. Ten days would pass and they would lie dead of starvation, and the treasure would be the property of him who had betrayed them. The men in the tomb were always conscious, therefore, of who it was that stood watch outside. Though it was the usual thing for a relative of someone inside the tomb to be drafted for the work, that was not always the safest procedure. There were wives who cursed husbands, sons who hated fathers. Ch'en's choice of his own wife and brother had much to recommend it to the others. Ch'en's young wife got along well with her husband, and she was a good-natured, amiable woman, pleasant to everyone. The brother had been reared like a son. He was of a wholesome nature such as to deny that he and Ch'en shared the same blood, and well thought of by everyone.

But it was not as wise a choice as the other thought it. The moment the two were alone the woman held out her hand to the man.

'Put the lid back on. Make up your mind to it. Go in and do it.'

She spoke in a low voice. The young man was startled. The same terrible thought had been with him from the moment he was appointed sentinel. He had been having an affair with the woman for a year and more. Though she was his brother's wife she did not seem like a sister-in-law. Ch'en had taken advantage of the fact that she was without resources, and had as good as kidnapped her, and had his way with her...

There was a rustling as the youth went off through the grass. The woman followed.

Yasushi Inoue, Princess Yung-t'ai's Necklace from Lou-lan and Other Stories, translated by James T Araki and Edward Seidensticker

YANG GUIFEI

Yang Guifei was a concubine whose love affair with Emperor Xuanzong of the Tang dynasty eventually brought about his downfall and the collapse of Xi'an's Golden Era. Her renowned beauty, and her power, have become legendary in China.

When Emperor Xuanzong had established a strong empire with a cosmopolitan capital at Chang'an (present-day Xi'an), he ordered a search throughout the land to find China's greatest beauty. Thousands of young women—one from as far away as Japan—are said to have been brought before him, only to be discarded or relegated to a secondary status in the back rooms of his palace.

One day, at Huaqing Hot Springs, Yang, the 18-year-old daughter of a high official and concubine of one of the emperor's many sons, caught Xuanzong's eye. Amidst protestations from his son, Xuanzong took Yang to be his own concubine, and she grew to wield enormous influence over the emperor, who began neglecting matters of state to spend time with her. He renamed her Yang Guifei—Yang the Imperial Concubine.

Tang-dynasty paintings indicate that—like other beauties of the time —Yang Guifei was as plump as a harem queen. Taking great pains to please her, the emperor had the palace at Huaqing Hot Springs enlarged, and she spent many languorous hours bathing there to keep her skin fresh. As the eminent Chinese poet Bai Juyi recounted:

> One cold spring day she was ordered
> To bathe in the Huaqing Palace baths,
> The warm water slipped down
> Her glistening jade-like body.
> When maids helped her rise
> She looked so frail and lovely,
> At once she won the emperor's favour...
> Behind the warm lotus-flower curtain,
> They took their pleasure in the spring nights,
> Regretting only that the nights were too short,

Rising only when the sun was high,
He stopped attending court sessions...
Constantly she amused and feasted with him,
Accompanying him on spring outings,
Spending every night with him.
Though many beauties were in the palace,
More than three thousand of them,
All his favours were centred on her.

(Translated by Yang Xianyi and Gladys Yang)

As Yang Guifei's spell over the emperor grew, so did her demands. Fresh lychees, her favourite fruit, were brought by pony express from the southern coastal city of Guangzhou every week. Many of her relatives took positions at court, with her cousin becoming Prime Minister.

Yang Guifei also caught the eye of a Mongolian Turk, An Lushan, who had become military governor in north China. Visiting the Tang court often, he was rumoured to have become Yang's lover. Although 15 years her elder, he was—in a bizarre ceremony—adopted as her son. An Lushan became impatient for power, and soon attempted a forceful take-over of the capital.

As his troops neared Xi'an, the emperor fled with Yang Guifei to the west. Years of neglect had weakened the imperial army, and its remaining soldiers were determined to remove Yang Guifei, whom they blamed for the military decline. When stopping to change horses at Mawei, the soldiers mutinied, killing the Prime Minister, and demanding that the 'moth-like eyebrows' of Yang Guifei be surrendered as well.

A more valiant lover might have given his own life first, but Xuanzong stood helplessly by as Yang Guifei was strangled in the courtyard of a small Buddhist temple.

The An Lushan rebellion dragged on for several years, but was eventually crushed. The emperor, however, never recovered from his loss of Yang Guifei, and he died a broken man a few years later. The Tang dynasty survived nominally, but a steady decline had set in, and its former glory was never regained.

EMPRESS WU

The Golden Age of the Tang dynasty was ushered in not by an emperor but by an ex-concubine, who became the only woman sovereign in Chinese history. Wu Zhou's remarkable career began in AD 638 when she entered the palace, aged 13, as junior concubine to Emperor Taizong. On his death 11 years later she was relegated to a Buddhist nunnery, as custom dictated, but by then—so it is traditionally alleged—she had already become the mistress of his son, Gaozong. She returned to court as Gaozong's favourite concubine, set about arranging the murder of the empress and other female rivals, and within a few years gained the rank of imperial consort for herself. Her ascendancy was not achieved without the ruthless dispatch of many opponents—ministers who had enjoyed the emperor's trust, members of the imperial family, and all those courtiers who claimed that her friendship with Gaozong was incestuous.

For much of Gaozong's long reign (AD 649–83) real power was in the hands of Empress Wu. She fully exploited his weakness and her own skill for intrigue. Purges of rivals—who were murdered or exiled—kept her position secure, but historians agree that it could not have been sustained had she not possessed great intelligence and a genius for administration. Although she was whimsical, superstitious and highly susceptible to the flattery of any sorcerer and monk who could win her favour, she remained for most of her rule consistently adept at picking competent statesmen and military leaders to carry out her policies. The conquest of Korea and defeat of the Turks were accomplished during her time. The imperial examination system—by which government officials were chosen regardless of social standing—was promoted, so that in time political power was transferred from the aristocracy to a scholar-bureaucracy. She was, as one historian put it, 'not sparing in the bestowal of titles and ranks, because she wished to cage the bold and enterprising spirits of all regions... but those who proved unfit for their responsibilities were forthwith, in large numbers, cashiered or executed. Her broad aim was to select men of real talent and true virtue.' During her years in power the stability of the empire laid the foundation for the prosperity and cultural achievements that followed and culminated in the High Tang.

Tri-colour glazed pottery figurine of a seated lady at her toilette (height 47.3cm), excavated from a Tang dynasty tomb. The décolleté neckline demonstrating the more daring fashions of the period

Empress Wu bore Gaozong four sons and one daughter. Their second son was named heir-apparent in AD 675 but Empress Wu, suspecting him of an attempted coup, banished the prince to Sichuan. It was there that he was subsequently made to take his own life, on his mother's orders. When the emperor died, another of Empress Wu's sons was enthroned. He proved to be as ineffectual as his father, and was speedily deposed and exiled as well. The reign of the next crown prince was equally short. In AD 690, Empress Wu dispensed with puppet emperors altogether by proclaiming a new dynasty—Zhou—and usurping the throne. Her title, Wu Zetian (Wu is Heaven), underscored her claim to the Mandate of Heaven.

While Wu Zetian continued to govern effectively, the last decade of her reign was overshadowed by several more savage murders. By now in her 70s, the old empress was becoming increasingly dependent on two corrupt courtiers, the Zhang brothers. Their malevolent presence was intensely loathed by the rest of the court, and it was insinuations against her favourites that impelled Wu Zetian to order the execution of her granddaughter, her step-grandson and another Wu relative on a charge of disloyalty. The Zhang brothers were finally killed in a palace coup in AD 705, which forced the empress to abdicate in favour of her exiled son and restore the Tang. She died less than a year later.

THE TOMB OF PRINCE YIDE

The tomb of Princess Yongtai's half-brother, who died at the age of 19, apparently executed for the same reason and at the same time as his half-sister, is dated the same year as hers, AD 706. Although the prince was unmarried when he died, his parents arranged a posthumous marriage for him and his 'wife' was buried with him at a later date. The tomb was excavated in 1970 and revealed some 1,600 figurines.

The layout of the tomb is much the same as that of Princess Yongtai, but in this case the walls are decorated with frescoes showing court ladies and eunuchs, palace guards and hunting attendants. There is also a long mural at the entrance with a 196-man procession of guards massed below the high watch-towers of Chang'an. The stone sarcophagus is slightly smaller, but similarly engraved.

The buildings in the pleasant garden courtyard house various examples of pottery figurines found in the tomb, including some fine tri-colour glazed figures on horseback and a superb, large tri-colour glazed horse.

THE TOMB OF THE HEIR-APPARENT PRINCE ZHANGHUAI

Prince Zhanghuai was one of Empress Wu's sons and he too fell foul of this formidable lady. He was heir-apparent from AD 675 to 680, but was then disgraced by his mother and banished to Sichuan Province, where he was forced to commit suicide in AD 684, at the age of 31. His younger brother later had the body exhumed and reburied here. The tomb was built in about AD 706. The two main paintings in the tomb are of a polo match on one side, and a hunting cavalcade on the other. There are also representations of foreign emissaries with court officials.

The two other tombs that have been opened are of the Prime Minister Xue Yuanzhao and General Li Jinxing, and are of lesser importance.

ZHAO LING

Zhao Ling is the tomb of Emperor Taizong, who founded the Tang dynasty. It is located in the main peak of Mount Jiuzong, approximately 60 kilometres (40 miles) northwest of Xi'an. Although 14 of the satellite tombs have been excavated, the emperor's mausoleum itself has not. The whole necropolis covers an area of some 200 square kilometres (77 square miles). Visitors are normally taken to see Zhao Ling Museum, but not the site on Mount Jiuzong itself.

Taizong was a great military commander who loved horses. Six bas-reliefs of his favourite mounts including his most famous horse, Quanmo, were originally placed at the northern entrance to the tomb. Considered masterpieces of Tang sculpture, they are unfortunately no longer *in situ*. The Quanmo stone, together with one other, was taken to the United States in 1914. The other four stones are in the Stone Sculpture Gallery of the Forest of Steles Museum, along with plaster reproductions of the two in America and are well worth a visit. The originals were sadly broken in several places in 1918, apparently in an attempt to facilitate their transport abroad.

The museum Zhao Ling displays all the artifacts removed from the excavated satellite tombs. There is a splendid selection of Tang funerary pottery, both glazed and unglazed, including figurines of Chinese and central Asians, horses and camels. There are some fragments of wall paintings, a ceremonial crown from a satellite tomb and a massive pottery roof finial from the Hall of Offerings, the main building of the original enclosure in front of the emperor's mausoleum.

There is also a selection of frescoes found in the satellite tombs. Although they are reproductions and poorly captioned, they are nonetheless splendid examples of Tang art and the costumes and fashions of the period. Those depicting dancers and musicians are especially delightful.

The museum also features a Forest of Steles (not to be confused with the famous one at Forest of Steles Museum in Xi'an). This is a collection of 42 vertical memorial tablets which originally stood outside the tomb mounds, together with ten black jade-stone tombstones from the interiors.

Unfortunately, the majority of the thousands of laboriously etched characters on these steles are illegible. They were damaged by vandals in the contemporary Tang and succeeding Song dynasties who, having made rubbings of the inscriptions, sought to inflate the value of their paper copies by defacing the source tablets.

XINGQING PARK

This is the largest park in Xi'an. Located east of the city wall's southeast corner opposite the Xi'an Jiaotong University, it is quiet and full of trees. On weekdays it is an excellent place to get away from the crowds.

The park was originally the site of a Tang palace, where the sons of Emperor Tang Ruizong (reigned AD 684–690 and AD 710–712) lived at the beginning of the eighth century. It became known as the Xingqing Palace in AD 714 after Emperor Xuanzong succeeded his father.

Famous for its peonies, Xingqing was a favourite palace of Emperor Xuanzong and Imperial Concubine Yang. After the Tang, the land on which the palace had been built eventually reverted to agricultural use.

The transformation of the site into a park came about in 1958 during the Great Leap Forward. Thousands of citizens were involved in laying out the park, taking only 120 days to complete the 50-hectare (123-acre) project.

It has an ornamental lake and a number of Tang-style buildings bearing the names of famous halls and pavilions in the palace of Xuanzong. There is also a white marble memorial, erected in 1979, to Abe no Nakamaro (AD 701–770), a famous secular Japanese visitor to Chang'an during the Tang, who rose to become Collator of Texts in the Imperial Library.

REMAINS OF DAMING PALACE

Daming Palace, or the Palace of Great Luminosity, was begun by Taizong in AD 634 for the use of his father, although Gaozu died before it was completed. In AD 663 it was enlarged for Emperor Gaozong and from then on became the principal palace of the Tang emperors.

The site of Daming Palace is to the northeast of the walled city, on the fringe of the modern urban area. The terraces on which once stood Hanyuan Hall (where important ceremonies were held) and Linde Hall (another large, but informal complex) may still be seen, together with a depression which was the ornamental Penglai Pool in Tang times. The whole area was excavated between 1957 and 1959, and the foundations of some 20 buildings were discovered. The Linde Hall in particular was completely excavated, although the site had now been filled in again.

THE TANG DYNASTY ARTS MUSEUM

Situated just around the corner from the Big Goose Pagoda, the Tang Dynasty Arts Museum is an offshoot of the Sino-Japanese joint venture hotel, the Xi'an Garden or Tanghua Fandian. It consists of four exhibition rooms.

Rooms one and two display a selection of reproduction frescoes and cultural relics recovered from various Tang-dynasty tombs. Room three is devoted to the theme of 'Chang'an—capital of the Tang Dynasty', with models of Daming Palace (see previous page) and the Little Goose Pagoda. A map of the city compares its layout with those of contemporary Rome, Alexandria in Egypt, Nara in Japan and shows how these cities were dwarfed by Chang'an at the time. There are also some

Reproduction of a mural originally decorating the tomb of Prince Zhanghuai. Showing foreign emissaries with Chinese court officials, it illustrates the cosmopolitan nature of Chang'an, ancient capital of the Tang dynasty (present-day Xi'an)

artifacts, including some bronze mirrors, demonstrating the prevailing style of dress, with interesting information on women's hairdos, make-up and clothing. Room four is the art gallery with a variety of original works by professors of Xi'an Art College. Monies from the sale of these paintings go to assist with the maintenance of the museum. A good selection of original art by the peasant painters of Huxian is also available (see page 136).

There is also a small shadow puppet theatre, where performances by the Shaanxi Folk Art Shadow Play Company are arranged for tour groups. Many examples of these colourful puppets, whose origin dates back to the Western Han dynasty, are for sale.

This is a place to enjoy relative peace and quiet amongst exhibition halls laid out between attractive gardens. it is open to the public 9 am–5 pm.

Buddhism during and after the Tang
Background

During the Tang, Chang'an became the main centre for Buddhist learning in east Asia. The first contacts between adherents of Buddhism and the Chinese were probably made with the opening of the Silk Road during the reign of the Martial Emperor, Han Wudi (reigned 140–86 BC). During the following centuries this central Asian route, with Chang'an at its eastern terminus, remained the principal one by which Buddhism reached China.

Today a number of monuments bear witness to the importance of Buddhism in the city's history. Most famous are the two prominent landmarks with unforgettable names: the Big and the Little Goose Pagodas (see pages 95 and 99). Also in reasonable condition is Da Cien Temple (of which the Big Goose Pagoda is a part), and two interesting temples south of the city, the Xingjiao and the Xiangji Temples (see pages 101 and 102). Some other Buddhist temples have survived in various states of disrepair but may prove worth visiting, as much for the setting and the journey there as for the temple buildings themselves.

Several of the surviving temples and pagodas have particular associations with Buddhist monks, scholars and translators who made the journey from Chang'an to India in search of enlightenment, the Buddhist scriptures and, perhaps, adventure. Some 200 Chinese monks are recorded as travelling from Chang'an to India between the third and eighth centuries. A number of central Asian and Indian monks also came to Chang'an, but they are less well documented than the Chinese travellers.

Of these monks the best known is Xuanzang who is today the most popular figure in the whole history of Chinese Buddhism. The Tang monk, as he is often simply called, is the hero of the long 16th-century Chinese novel *Pilgrimage to the West*, sometimes known as *Monkey*, which is loosely based on Xuanzang's travels. A scholar and translator, Xuanzang made a 17-year journey which took him to Nalanda (near Patna), then the greatest centre of Buddhist learning in India.

In his return he became abbot of Da Cien Temple (see below), where he spent the rest of his life working on translations of the Buddhist texts that he had brought with him from India. His remains were interred under a pagoda which is part of the Xingjiao Temple (see page 101).

By the early eighth century, Chang'an had a total of 64 monasteries and 27 nunneries. Much of the scholarship that resulted in the development of two important Buddhist sects—Pure Land and True Word—took place in the city. But the monasteries fulfilled a number of different roles, not only translating, studying and propagating religion, but also patronizing the arts, providing accommodation and even offering some banking facilities. They grew extremely rich, and Buddhism began to enjoy immense popularity at every level of society.

The Tang emperors, however, were ambivalent in their support of the foreign religion. They claimed that Laozi, the founder of China's indigenous religion Daoism, was their ancestor. Increasingly the success of the great temple-monasteries provoked resistance, and attempts were made to limit their power and wealth. Finally in AD 841 came a crackdown: the insane Daoist Emperor Tang Wuzong ordered the dissolution of the monasteries and the return of monks and nuns to secular life. During the following four years, widespread Buddhist persecution led to the destruction of almost all the temple-monasteries. Though many of them were re-established after AD 845, and some of them survive to this day, Buddhism never completely recovered in China. And so, after the destruction of Chang'an at the end of the Tang, the city lost its position as a centre of Buddhist learning for good.

Sights

THE BIG GOOSE PAGODA AND DA CIEN TEMPLE

The Big Goose Pagoda (Dayan Ta), perhaps the most beautiful building left in Xi'an today, is one of the city's most distinctive and outstanding landmarks. The adjacent Da Cien Temple is the city's best-preserved Buddhist temple complex.

Situated four kilometres (two-and-a-half miles) south of the walled city at the end of Yanta Lu, or Goose Pagoda Road, the temple and pagoda are on the sites of an earlier Sui temple. Da Cien Temple was established in AD 647 by Li Zhi (who became Emperor Tang Gaozong in AD 649) in memory of his mother Empress Wende.

ON CLIMBING THE BIG GOOSE PAGODA IN CHANG'AN

At the top of the pagoda one feels
To have truly entered the sky;
Wind drums incessantly; I am
Not one free of care and here my worry increases;
And this structure,
Representing the power of Buddha,
Makes one wish to understand
And penetrate the depths of his secrets;
Looking through the dragon and snake
Openings, one marvels at their intricacy
Of construction; the seven
Stars come into view and the Milky Way;
One knows that the sun has been forced down,
And that it is autumn already; clouds
Obscure the mountain; the waters
Of the clear Wei and the muddy Ching
Seem to have come together; below us
Is the mist, so can one hardly realize
Down there lies our capital;
There is a hardly-to-be-defined air
Near the grave of the ancient Emperor Shun,
And one cries for his awakening; but now
By the Jade Lake, the Queen of the Western
Heavens disports herself with wine, as
The sun sets behind Mount Kunlun
And yellow cranes fly aimlessly,
While the wild geese stream into
The sunset, searching for life.

Du Fu (712–770)

*Written by Du Fu while on an excursion with some other poets to the Pagoda
of Kindness and Grace, better known now as the Dayan Ta or Big Goose Pagoda.*

The seven-storey Big Goose Pagoda

Completed in AD 652, the pagoda was built at the request of the Tang monk, Xuanzang, whose pilgrimage to India is immortalized in the 16th-century Chinese novel *Pilgrimage to the West* or *Monkey*. Xuanzang asked Emperor Gaozong to build a large stone stupa like those he had seen on his travels. The emperor offered a compromise brick structure of five storeys, about 53 metres (174 feet) high, which was completed in AD 652. Originally called the Scripture Pagoda, it is said to be where Xuanzang translated into Chinese the Buddhist scriptures he brought back from India. Its present name, Big Goose Pagoda, has never been satisfactorily explained.

Between AD 701 and AD 704, at the end of the reign of Empress Wu, five more storeys were added to the pagoda, giving a sharper, more pointed form than it has today. Later damage, probably by fire, reduced it to the seven storeys it now has. It is a simple, powerful, harmonious structure, although ironically not how Xuanzang wanted it to be.

The pagoda rises 64 metres (210 feet) to the north of the other temple buildings, and is the only remaining Tang building in the complex. On the pedestal, at the entrance to the first storey, are some rather faded photographs providing a useful and fascinating survey of other famous pagodas in China, as well as a number of Tang inscriptions and engravings set in the base of the pagoda. There are some delightful tendril designs in bas-relief on the borders of the tablets and at the top of the tablets some exquisite coiling dragons and singing angels.

At the southern entrance of the pagoda are copies of prefaces to the translations of Xuanzang by the emperors Taizong and Gaozong in the calligraphy of Chu Sui-liang. Over the lintel of the western entrance is an engraving of Sakyamuni and other Buddhist figures. Some tablets, inscribed during the Ming (1368–1644), recount the exploits of the Tang monk. On a fine day climb up inside the internal wooden staircase to the top of the pagoda for a panoramic view.

During the Tang, Da Cien Temple was a considerable establishment. There were about 300 resident monks and no fewer than 1,897 rooms around 13 courtyards. It contained paintings by the leading artists of the day, and had the finest peony garden in the capital.

Although the temple was one of four to continue functioning after the great Buddhist persecution of AD 841–845, it was destroyed at the end of the Tang (AD 907). Since then it has been ruined and restored several times, but on a diminished scale. The last major restoration occurred in 1954, when the pagoda pedestal was widened.

The temple entrance is on the south side. Inside, to the right and left, are the Bell and Drum Towers, and a path leading to the Great Hall. This contains three statues of buddhas, surrounded by 18 clay figures of Sakyamuni Buddha's disciples. Both the building and the statues inside are said to date from 1466. In front of the

Scripture Library is a stone lamp from the Japanese city of Kyoto. To the east of the Great Hall are several small stone pagodas marking the remains of monks of the Qing period (1644–1911). Some new temple buildings are being constructed behind the pagoda. Built in Tang style around a courtyard, they will serve as a monument to monk Xuanzang and house Buddhist scriptures and details of his life and achievements. The complex is scheduled to open some time in 2000.

The temple is open from 8.30 am to 5.30 pm. Just around the corner is the Tang Arts Museum (see page 93)

THE LITTLE GOOSE PAGODA AND DA JIANFU TEMPLE

The Little Goose Pagoda (Xiaoyan Ta) is one of Xi'an's major landmarks. Situated to the south of the walled city, the 13-storey eighth-century pagoda is all that remains of the once flourishing Da Jianfu Temple. The temple, established in AD 684 in honour of Emperor Gaozong, was particularly associated with pilgrim Yijing, who settled there in the early eighth century to translate texts he had brought back from India. Although the temple continued to function after the Buddhist persecutions of AD 841–845, everything was destroyed save the Little Goose Pagoda, and an old locust tree said to have been planted during the Tang. Later, more modest temple buildings were erected next to the pagoda.

The pagoda has not survived completely unscathed. When it was completed in AD 707 the brick structure had 15 storeys, but it was damaged during a series of earthquakes in the late 15th and 16th centuries. In 1487, the pagoda was split from top to bottom by the impact of an earthquake measuring 6.25 on the Richter scale. Amazingly, it did not fall. In 1556 another quake, 8 on the Richter scale, had its epicentre some 75 kilometres (47 miles) east of Xi'an. This one had the effect of throwing the two sides of the pagoda together again, but it also dislodged the top two storeys.

The Little Goose Pagoda has remained to this day only 13 storeys, 43 metres (141 feet) high. There have been conflicting opinions about the original appearance of the building, which is partly why a complete restoration has never been attempted. (Drawings of the different designs are on display, alongside photographs of the restoration work, in a pavilion beside the pagoda. There are also dramatic photographs showing the temple rent in two following the earthquake.) Meanwhile, however, the slightly crumbling, open part of its apex gives it a distinct style. A new internal staircase was put up in 1965 so you can climb to the top. Unlike the Big Goose Pagoda, which has only narrow windows, here you can climb out to an open roof to enjoy an untrammelled view of the surroundings.

Among the noteworthy features of the pagoda are some Tang-period engravings of bodhisattvas on the stone lintels at its base. There is also a tablet commemorating

a restoration of the pagoda in 1116 and another engraved during the Qing (1644–1911) with information about the earthquakes. A stone table dated 1692 gives an interesting idea of what the temple and pagoda would have looked like at that date, except that the pagoda is represented with 15 storeys.

Standing in one of the courtyards behind the pagoda is a small Bell Tower, housing a large bell measuring 3.55 metres (11.6 feet) high and weighing 8,000 kilograms (over 17,000 pounds). It was cast in 1192 in Wugong County, west of Xi'an and moved to the temple about five centuries later. Beside it is a modern replica which can be struck by visitors for a small fee. Opposite the Bell Tower is the Drum Tower. Traditionally a Buddhist monk struck a bell before noon and a drum in the afternoon and evening.

It is worth visiting the exhibition rooms of Shaanxi handicrafts at this pagoda. The Little Goose pagoda is open from 8.30 am to 5.30 pm.

XINGJIAO TEMPLE

This temple is in a very pleasant setting, overlooking the Fanchuan River, 22 kilometres (14 miles) southeast of Xi'an, just beyond the village of Duqu. Xingjiao Temple, or the Temple of the Flourishing Teaching, was one of the Eight Great Temples of Fanchuan. It was built in AD 669 by Tang Gaozong as a memorial to the Tang monk Xuanzang (see page 95), together with a tall brick pagoda covering his ashes. The temple was restored in AD 828, though by AD 839 it again lay abandoned according to the inscription on Xuanzang's pagoda. However, it managed to survive until the 19th century when all the buildings were destroyed except the main pagoda and two smaller ones belonging to two of Xuanzang's disciples. The temple was again rebuilt, partly in 1922, partly in 1939. Today, over 30 monks live and worship there.

The three pagodas stand in a walled enclosure called Cien Pagoda Courtyard. The tall central pagoda is dedicated to Xuanzang. It is a beautiful five-storey brick structure, with brackets in relief, in imitation of the old wooden-style pagodas. It probably dates from the ninth century. A small pavilion next to the pagoda has a modern copy of a stone engraving of Xuanzang, carrying the scriptures in what might be described as a sutra-backpack.

On either side of the principal pagoda are those of Xuanzang's two translation assistants. Each is of three storeys. On the east side is that of Kuiji (AD 632–682), nephew of General Yuchi Jingde (a general of Emperor Tang Taizong). It was erected during the Tang. On the other side stands the pagoda of Yuance, a Korean follower of Xuanzang. This was built later, in 1115.

At the entrance to the complex are the Bell and Drum Towers. These are 20th century constructions but retain the original instruments from the 19th century or

The Little Goose Pagoda, built in the eighth century, was split in two by an earthquake in 1487. Another more violent quake in 1556 threw the two sides together again. It has since been restored

earlier. Facing the entrance is the Great Hall of the Buddha, built in 1939, which contains a bronze, Ming-period Buddha. The Preaching Hall behind was built in 1922 and contains a number of statues including a bronze, Ming-period Amitabha Buddha and a Sakyamuni Buddha of the same date as the hall.

In the eastern courtyard is the two-storey library, built in 1922 and restored in 1939. It contains a white jade Buddha from Burma. The library proper is on the upper floor and possesses some Tang-dynasty sutras, written in Sanskrit, as well as 20th-century editions of the great Tang translations of Xuanzang and others.

You can reach the temple by bus number 215 that leaves from Xi'an's South Gate. The trip takes about 40 minutes.

DAXINGSHAN TEMPLE

Daxingshan Temple was the greatest Buddhist establishment of the Sui and Tang, but since the tenth century it has been destroyed and rebuilt several times. The last reconstruction was in 1956. In 1999, the buildings around the front courtyard were either completely reconstructed or extensively renovated and some of the main temple buildings have recently been repainted. A number of monks live and worship there. The temple complex and stands in well-wooded, peaceful surroundings and is more extensive than it at first seems.

The temple is said to date back to the third century when it was known as the Zunshan Temple. It was refounded during the Sui when it was given its present name, and became the headquarters of an order with a network of 45 prefectural temples, all established by Yang Qian, founder of the Sui dynasty. During the Tang it became a great centre of Buddhist art and learning and the Tang monk, Xuanzang, hero of the famous Chinese novel *Monkey*, stayed there during the seventh century. Most of the buildings were destroyed during the Buddhist persecution of 841–845, and whatever survived disappeared at the end of the Tang. The temple was rebuilt under the Ming and again restored in 1785 by an expert on Tang-dynasty Chang'an called Bi Yuan (1730–97). After its reconstruction in 1956 it was used by a community of Lamaist monks until the Cultural Revolution (1966–76). Today it houses the Xi'an Buddhist Association.

The temple is located south of the Little Goose Pagoda on a small street called Xingshan Si Jie, near the open market of Xiaozhai.

XIANGJI TEMPLE

Xiangji Temple, which has an 11-storey pagoda built in AD 706, lies due south of Xi'an some 20 kilometres (12 miles), close to the town of Wangqu. The square brick pagoda was built over the ashes of the Buddhist Shandao, one of the patriarchs of Pure Land Buddhism which preached salvation through faith rather than meditation.

It was built by a disciple named Jingye, who is himself commemorated by a small five-storey brick pagoda nearby. Around the pagodas were originally the buildings of one of the great temple-monasteries of Tang Chang'an, although these have long since disappeared.

The pagoda of Shandao is similar in some respects to that of Xuanzang at the Temple of Flourishing Teaching. It has brackets in relief and imitates a wooden structure. If you want to climb the pagoda, try persuading one of the monks for permission. There are about 25 monks who now live and worship at the temple.

On 14 May 1980, which was, by Chinese reckoning, the 1,300th anniversary of Shandao's death in AD 681, a major restoration of the temple was completed. The Great Hall of the Buddha was rebuilt, and a Japanese Buddhist delegation presented a figure of the monk Shandao. It is now on view inside the hall together with a figure of Amitabha Buddha which was brought from a Beijing museum.

It is difficult to reach the temple by bus and a taxi is the most realistic option. But the beautiful surrounding countryside and, of course, the pagodas themselves make the trip well worthwhile.

CAOTANG TEMPLE

Sometimes translated as the Straw Hut Temple, Caotang Temple was founded during the Tang. Surrounded by fields, it lies about 55 kilometres (34 miles) southwest of Xi'an.

The temple was built on the side of a palace where Kumarajiva, a fourth-century translator of Buddhist scriptures, once worked and taught. Kumarajiva's translations, known for their elegant style rather than for their accuracy, have been used continuously down to modern times. The ashes of Kumarajiva are beneath a stone stupa, thought to be Tang, about two metres (6.5 feet) high, inside a small pavilion. In front there are some old cypress trees and a well. Other temple buildings include bell and tablet pavilions and a main hall.

The temple is on the road to Huxian and accessible by taxi or long-distance bus.

HUAYAN TEMPLE

Huayan Temple was founded by the first patriarch of the Huayan sect of Buddhism, the monk Dushan (AD 557–640), during the reign of Tang Taizong. In its heyday, the temple, situated in the Fanchuan area 20 kilometres (12 miles) south of Xi'an, was one of the Eight Great Temples of Fanchuan which flourished during the Tang.

Today, the only part of the temple to have survived are two brick pagodas on the side of the hill. One of them is 23 metres (75 feet) high and is square, like the Big Goose Pagoda, with seven storeys; the other is small with four storeys and is hexagonal in form. There is a good view of the surrounding area from the pagodas.

Located on the road that passes through Chang'an, southeast of Xi'an, the pagodas are accessible by bus number 215 that leaves from the South Gate (a trip of about 45 minutes) and can be visited conveniently on the way to Xingjiao Temple.

THE TEMPLE OF THE RECUMBENT DRAGON

The Temple of the Recumbent Dragon (Wo Long Si), believed to have been built during the Eastern Han in about 168 AD, was served by some 300 monks during the Ming dynasty (1368–1644). The name apparently comes from the fact that the emperor Zhao Kuangyin (the dragon always symobolized the emperor), who founded the Song dynasty in 960, enjoyed coming to this temple to rest and play chess with the monks. It suffered particularly badly during the Cultural Revolution (1966–76), when virtually all the artwork was destroyed as everything but the strongest walls and foundations were razed.

For almost two decades the temple site was used to house a factory. Since 1982, three quarters of the floor area has been returned to the temple's jurisdiction in compliance with Government policy promoting freedom of religious beliefs. About 80 monks now stay at the temple, and three large halls and several peripheral structures have been built, one of which is a dining hall.

Access to the temple is down a lane between numbers 25 and 27 Baishulin Jie, a five-minute walk from the Forest of Steles Museum. Walk straight out of the museum gate to Baishulin Jie, turn left and take the second lane on the right.

GUANGREN TEMPLE

The Guangren Temple is a Lama temple, located on Xibei Yi Lu within the north-westernmost corner of the city wall. It is one of only four such temples outside Tibet, the others being the Labrang Lamasery in southern Gansu, the Ta'er Lamasery in Qinghai, and the Lama Temple in Beijing. This temple, however, is by no means as grand as its cousins. Built in 1705 during the Qing dynasty, Guangren Temple functioned as a place of worship and lodging for monks and pilgrims travelling between Beijing and Tibet. According to the monks now serving at the temple, the Dalai Lama himself once stayed here briefly in 1952.

As with most religious sites during the catastrophic Cultural Revolution, Guangren Temple suffered from officially sanctioned destruction by Red Guards. The old east section is still occupied by a factory, although there is talk about possibly one day restoring this, and the front courtyard is partly occupied by another building. All this makes the temple appear quite small and insignificant on entering the gate, particularly as it stands in the shadow of the imposing Ming city wall. However, appearances are deceptive and there are three main courtyards tucked away behind the first hall.

Calligraphy on a stele housed in a pavilion in the front courtyard was written by Kangxi, the second Qing emperor. The name plaque over the entrance to the main hall also bears his calligraphy, while inside the hall itself hang two lamps that were gifts to the temple from the Empress Dowager Cixi.

To get there by bus, take the number 10 running west along Lianhu Lu and alight at Yuxiang Men. Walk back east along Lianhu Lu, turn left into Xibei Yi Lu and the temple is right at the end of the street against the wall.

FAMEN TEMPLE

Famen Temple is situated some 118 kilometres (73 miles) west of Xi'an, at a site on the Silk Road en route to Baoji, Tianshui and Lanzhou. It will thus appeal to travellers who are journeying west to retrace that ancient trade route, or indeed those visitors to Xi'an who can fit Famen Temple into a day's tour to the west which also encompasses Qian Ling. Others may consider that the opportunity of seeing a supposed finger bone of the founder of Buddhism warrants a special day trip in itself. Though it said that only a reproduction is on display, while the genuine item is locked securely away.

The origins of the Famen temple can be traced back to the Eastern Han dynasty, between AD 147 and 189, although its pagoda, a handsome 47-metre (154-foot) high greyish-white brick octagonal structure with 13 levels, actually dates from Ming times.

About a century after the death of Sakyamuni, the founder of Buddhism, the ancient Indian King Ashoka decided to distribute a selection of Sakyamuni's relics to many places in the known world where Buddhism had gained adherents. Famen Temple was awarded a relic, a single finger bone. The original stupa was built in 532 AD during the Northern Wei dynasty. During the Tang dynasty, the stupa was rebuilt and the relic stored in a crypt beneath it. A succession of emperors and their concubines either came to Famen themselves or had the relic taken to Chang'an. It was during this time that the temple gained nationwide fame. Later, when Buddhism was under wide attack (see page 95), an imperial edict ordered that the finger bone of Sakyamuni be destroyed, but the relic was hidden by the monks.

Although the Tang stupa was destroyed, a 13-storey octagonal pagoda was built on the site during the Ming dynasty. It was completed in 1609, having taken 37 years to build. The original Tang crypt remained untouched and the relic believed to be lost.

On 24 August 1981, the Ming pagoda partially collapsed, leaving exactly half the structure standing and the other half a pile of rubble. It was only during the reconstruction work in 1987 that eight caskets containing four finger bones were discovered in the crypt beneath the pagoda's foundation. Only one of these is believed to be original, while the others are Tang reproductions.

All these bones (tiny, white in colour and tubular in shape), the jewel-encrusted previous metal caskets in which they were found, and hosts of other relics discovered at Famen are now on display in the Treasure Hall of the temple.

The temple complex houses a working monastery, with over 40 monks in residence. It has been faithfully reconstructed from original Tang drawings. The solid pagoda is set in pleasant garden surroundings tended by the monks, and very competently so judging by the size of the pumpkins and cabbages. Beyond the pagoda stands the Bell Tower and Drum Tower. At first glance these, and the Treasure Hall next door, appear reminiscent of Japanese architecture. Until, that is, one is reminded that Japan was greatly influenced by China during the Tang dynasty, and some of the best surviving examples of Tang architecture today are to be found in Japan.

A set of stairs in front of the pagoda leads to the recently renovated crypt—the largest pagoda crypt ever found in China. Lined with white marble and brightly lit, it is far from atmospheric. The finger bone is displayed behind a glass window, set in a tiny gold pavilion as it was originally found. Whether this is a reproduction or not, one cannot help thinking that Sakyamuni must have had rather large hands. A small part of the original crypt has been preserved, however, and is on display behind another window at floor level. It is laid out with various stone statues and scripture tablets.

Of great interest to many visitors to the temple will undoubtedly be the relics on display in the museum. However, because of their enormous archaeological or religious importance, a number of these treasures are often away on tour either in China or overseas, leaving only photographs in their place. You should see at least some, if not all of the set of eight caskets, originally nested one inside another, that contained the finger bone. They are made of gold or silver and some set with precious stones, with an outer box of sandalwood. There are also various other magnificent examples of Tang gold and silver ware, demonstrating the advanced metalworking techniques and skills of the craftsmen of that period. Examples include a gilded silver bowl with an overlapping lotus petal design; the four gilded silver *yanjia* (the ritual vessels for the consecration of the image of Buddha), found in the four corners of the crypt; an exquisite gilded silver basket with an open-work design decorated with geese in flight; eight small gilded silver plates with a peony design.

New exhibition rooms are being constructed to provide improved facilities to exhibit these relics to the some 300,000 visitors that the temple receives annually. These should be open in July 2000.

Those wishing to stay overnight in Famen can do so at the Famen Temple Hotel, a short distance down the road from the temple (turn right out of the temple gate). See Hotels section on page 146.

FUNERARY FINERY

In a large grey building standing to one side of the Drum Tower, under a line of Chinese characters painted to read 'Municipal Theatre Costume Retail Department', there was a door with a curious sign on its lintel. It said: 'Funeral and Interment Clothes Sold Here'. The door was closed, but you could get into the shop by either one of two additional entrances; these had signs which said, 'Men's and Women's Fashions', and 'Theatrical Costumes, Props and Dance Costumes'.

I thought that this was worth more than a moment of my curiosity, and stepped into the darkness of the building. I made for the funeral clothes counter, which turned out to be in the far end of the shop. It was very dark there, but still it was not difficult to see the sign pinned up above the counter, which said, 'Burial suits, once sold, are without exception not returnable'. I asked to see one.

She took a minute to look through her stock—from where I stood I could see that she was plentifully supplied—and came up with something which I thought you nowadays only saw in the movies. It took my breath away, it was so sumptuous, a beautiful ensemble in silk, such as might have been worn by a court lady in the Qing dynasty. The robe was of purple silk, deep as the skin of an aubergine, and trimmed with a border of gold. The skirt, of a heavier silk, was midnight blue and splashed with a phoenix pattern embroidered in gold. (I supposed that the male version would be a dragon). Together the pieces cost 32 yuan, well over half of an average wage earner's monthly salary.

In such finery are the richer dead arrayed when they go to their graves in China. How incorrigible they are, those millions of Chinese in their baggy blue suits; if they don't dress very stylishly when they are alive they certainly make up for it when they die. And the thought came to me that all the chic, all the colour, all the money of China is expended on the children and the dead.

Lynn Pan, China's Sorrow, 1985

SWISS EFFICIENCY

*S*ian *is remarkable for its rickshaws. They have blue or white hood-covers, embroidered with big flowers, of an oddly Victorian design. We used the rickshaws a good deal, out of laziness, despite Dr Mooser's warning that their upholstery often contained typhus-lice. Typhus is one of the great scourges of Shen-si Province. One of Mooser's two colleagues, an engineer, went down with it soon after his arrival, but, thanks to an inoculation, the attack was comparatively slight.*

Dr Mooser himself was a stocky figure, eagle-eyed with a bitter mouth and a smashed, rugged face. He wore a leather jerkin, riding-breeches, and big strapped boots. He rushed at life, at China, at his job, with his head down, stamping and roaring like a bull. The dishonesty and laziness of the average Chinese official was driving him nearly frantic. 'While I'm here,' he bellowed at his assistants, 'you are all Swiss. When I go away you can be Chinese again, if you like—or anything else you Goddam well please.'

Not that Mooser had much use for his countrymen either, or, indeed, for any Europeans at all. 'The Swiss are crooks, the Germans are crooks, the English are the damn lousiest crooks of the lot... It was you lousy bastards who wouldn't let ambulances be sent to China. I have all the facts. I shall not rest until they are published in the newspaper.' With his colleagues he spoke Swiss dialect, or English—boycotting High German, the language of the Nazis.

Dr Mooser had established several refugee camps in Sian, as well as a delousing station. The refugees were housed in empty buildings. As soon as could be arranged they were sent off into the country and distributed amongst the neighbouring villages. There were about eight thousand of them in the city, including one thousand Mohammedans, who had a special camp to themselves. These people belonged mostly to the middle class of China—nearly all of them had a little money. The really poor had no choice but to stay where they were, and await the coming of the Japanese. The really rich were already safe in Hong Kong.

(preceding pages) Rapeseed and wheat fields outside Xi'an. Farmers in the region plant two crops per year—maize from July to October and winter wheat from November to June.

There was no doubt of Mooser's efficiency. The camps were well run, the floors and bedding clean, the children's faces washed, and there was hardly any spitting. Mooser was a great favourite with the children. Whenever he visited them his pockets were full of sweets. 'I had to sack three camp commandants in the first week,' he told us. 'They call me The Chaser.'

Mooser didn't quite know what to make of us—especially after he had heard from me that Auden was a poet. He had no use for poetry because 'it changes the order of the words'. While he was working in Mexico he was summoned to the bedside of an Englishman named David H Lawrence, 'a queer-looking fellow with a red beard. I told him: "I thought you were Jesus Christ." And he laughed. There was a big German woman sitting beside him. She was his wife. I asked him what his profession was. He said he was a writer. "Are you a famous writer?" I asked him. "Oh no," he said. "Not so famous." His wife didn't like that. "Didn't you really know my husband was a writer?" she said to me. "No," I said. " Never heard of him." And Lawrence said: "Don't be silly, Frieda. How should he know I was a writer? I didn't know he was a doctor, either, till he told me."

Dr Mooser then examined Lawrence and told him that he was suffering from tuberculosis—not from malaria, as the Mexican doctor had assured him. Lawrence took it very quietly. He only asked how long Mooser thought he would live. 'Two years,' said Mooser. 'If you're careful.' This was in 1928.

W H Auden and Christopher Isherwood, Journey to a War, 1939

Dr Mooser and his two Swiss colleagues, of the League of Nations Commission, were advising the Chinese government on the prevention of infectious diseases.

Village life—cave-style houses dug out of loess embankments can still be seen in many areas of the Xi'an countryside

Period Five: Medieval and Modern Xi'an
Background

With the destruction of Chang'an at the end of the Tang, the city lost its political splendour and power for good. Thereafter it remained a regional centre, usually out of the mainstream of political developments. The real economic centre of China had already moved away from Chang'an, further to the southwest, during the late Tang. After AD 907 the Xi'an area became progressively more impoverished and culturally backward. Much of the history in the following millennium is a dismally repetitious account of droughts and floods, famines and peasant insurrections.

However, Daoism continued to find adherents and remnants of Daoist temples (see page 127) can be seen in Xi'an today, despite the destruction caused during the Cultural Revolution. Islam, which had first been introduced into Chang'an by Arab merchants during the Tang, also flourished. Xi'an's beautiful Great Mosque is still functioning and welcomes foreign visitors (see page 126).

Between the fall of the Tang and the establishment of the Ming dynasty in 1368, the city changed its name many times. In 1368 the city was renamed Xi'an Fu, the Prefecture of Western Peace. It was to remain as Xi'an from then on, except for the last year of the Ming dynasty (1644), when the peasant leader Li Zicheng captured the city and renamed it Chang'an. (The name Chang'an survives today as the name of the county town immediately south of Xi'an).

THE MING DYNASTY

In 1370 Zhu Yuanzhang, the first emperor of the Ming dynasty, put his second son, Zhu Shuang, in control of Xi'an. Zhu Shuang became Prince of Qin, using the old name for the area. A palace was constructed for him and the city substantially rebuilt on the site of the Imperial City section of the Tang capital, covering approximately one sixth of the original area. The prince did not take up residence until 1378, when the palace and the walls and gates of the city had already been completed. Although the palace, which was in the northeast part of the city, no longer exists, part of 14th-century Xi'an still survives, notably the Bell and Drum towers and the city wall and gates.

THE QING DYNASTY

When the Manchus established the last imperial dynasty of China, the Qing, in 1644, Xi'an was garrisoned by Manchu troops. They occupied the northeast section of the city, which was walled off. In European accounts, these soldiers were referred to inaccurately, as 'Tartars'.

During the 18th century the city, or at least its officials and merchants, enjoyed some prosperity, as indicated by the great development of Qingqiang opera at his time (see page 35). However, the 19th century was less happy with natural calamities following fast on the heels of a disastrous Muslim rebellion (1862–73).

In 1900 Xi'an again became a capital of sorts during the Boxer Rebellion when the Empress Dowager Cixi (1835–1908), with her captive nephew, the powerless Emperor Guangxu, fled in disguise from Beijing. They stayed for over a year in Xi'an, beyond the reach of the Western powers, while peace was negotiated.

In 1911 when a nationwide revolution overthrew the Qing regime, resistance by the garrison in Xi'an collapsed without much of a struggle. But a terrible massacre of the Manchus ensued. Between 10,000 and 20,000 were killed, including a few unlucky foreigners. Most of the buildings in the Manchu quarter were burned down. Such blood-letting and destruction did not occur in other cities. Much of the killing in Xi'an was evidently led by the Muslims, in revenge for the suppression of their rebellion 40 years earlier.

XI'AN IN REPUBLICAN ERA

During the Republican period of 1911 to 1949 Xi'an gradually became less isolated from the outer world. Before the revolution the city had already established its first telegraph office (in 1885) and international post office (in 1902). The railway did not reach Xi'an until 1934, but Westerners started to visit the city in increasing numbers from the turn of the century onwards, usually making contact with the China Inland Mission, the Scandinavian Alliance Mission or the English Baptists, all of whom were represented in the city. They returned, frequently to write books, informing (and often misinforming) the outside world about 'ancient Sian-fu':

> It will be long before the city of Western Peace becomes the resort of sightseers. Yet Sian and its neighbourhood provide more sights to see than most inland Chinese capitals, in case the blessed day of trains de luxe and steam-heated hotels should ever draw for it. The rolling plain, all round as far as you can see, is full of mounds and barrows; and two noble pagodas invite inspection. Or you can mount the wall and study the whole flat extent of the city; you can ascend the Drum Tower, and from the vast darkness of its loft look out towards the turquoise roofs of the Mahometan mosque, and beyond these, to the orange gables of the Imperial Palace, where the Grand Dowager pitched her flying tents in 1900.

> (From *On the Eaves of the World* by Reginald Farrar, 1917)

During the struggle for power in the 1920s and '30s, Xi'an was of some strategic importance and once again in its history played a dramatic role: in 1926, it was occupied by a pro-Nationalist Shaanxi general, Yang Hucheng, and was promptly surrounded by an anti-Nationalist force. So began the six-month Siege of Xi'an. When it was finally lifted, some 50,000 were said to have died. Revolution Park marks the place where they were buried (see page 134).

In the struggle between communist and Nationalist forces, Xi'an came to the forefront in 1936, when Huaqing Hot Springs was the scene of the so-called Xi'an Incident (see page 130). Chiang Kai-shek, intent on getting rid of domestic communist opposition before putting up resistance to the invading Japanese, was arrested by two Nationalist generals, Yang Hucheng and the leader of the displaced Northeastern Army, Zhang Xueliang, and forced to agree to join the communists against the common enemy, the Japanese. Xi'an became a vital link between the communist headquarters in Yan'an and the outside world through the establishment of the Eighth Route Army Office (see page 134).

During the Sino-Japanese War, Xi'an was bombed, but never occupied by the Japanese. After the war, the city was controlled by Nationalist troops until it was taken by communist forces on 20 May 1949. The People's Republic of China was inaugurated less than five months later.

XI'AN UNDER THE PEOPLE'S REPUBLIC

Xi'an has grown much larger in the past 40 years, both in size and population. Many new industries have also been established. The initial impetus for this growth came from the Government whose policy was to give priority to the development of the cities in the interior.

In 1949 Xi'an did not extend much farther than the walled city, covering only 13.2 square kilometres (5 square miles). Today the city has spread to 100 square kilometres (38.6 square miles), an extent even larger than the Tang capital of Chang'an which occupied an area of 81 square kilometres (31.3 square miles) within the outer walls. The modern city is not so regular in its layout as its great predecessor, and it extends further to the east and west than the Tang city.

The population has increased rapidly since the 1930s when it was between 200,000 and 300,000. Today it is 5.4 million in the metropolitan area, including people living both within the urban area and the outlying farming villages.

Sights

THE FOREST OF STELES (BEILIN) MUSEUM

The Forest of Steles Museum was formally established in 1952 and occupies the former Temple of Confucius along the inside of the southern section of the city wall, on Baishulin Jie. It used to be the principal museum for Shaanxi and displayed antiquities brought from every part of the province, but the exhibits shown to illustrate the history of Shaanxi have now been transferred to the new National Museum of Shaanxi History (see page 120) which opened in July 1991.

The famous collection of over 1,000 inscribed stones known as the Forest of Steles began in 1090 when a large Confucian collection of steles cut in AD 837—the oldest existing texts of the Confucian classics—was moved for safekeeping to the back of the Temple of Confucius. The collection slowly grew until by the 18th century it was already called by its present name. It is the largest collection of its kind in China.

The art of inscribing on stone began in China at least as early as the fourth century BC. The earliest examples that have survived from this time are the ten Stone Drums of Qin. Recording a hunting party led by a Duke of Qin, they were discovered during the Tang dynasty at Fengxiang, about 145 kilometres (90 miles) west of Xi'an. The originals are now in Beijing but a reproduction of one of them is on display in the Shaanxi History Museum.

From the Han dynasty onwards flat stones were cut with either text or pictures, not only for commemorative purposes but also to make it possible to reproduce them on paper by taking rubbings. These rubbings, made into either scrolls or books, often serve as models for calligraphy practice.

A stone rubbing being made at the Forest of Steles Museum. A sheet of damp paper is first placed on the stone and allowed to dry and then pounded with a pad of tightly wrapped cloth soaked in ink

As a rough guide, the contents of the Forest of Steles can be divided into four groups: works of literature and philosophy, historical records, calligraphy and pictorial stones. Of most immediate interest are the pictorial stones in Room Four, which are displayed with some stones engraved with historical records. They are almost all relatively late, from the Ming (1368–1644) or Qing (1644–1911). As well as landscapes and portraits—notably of Confucius and Bodhidarma—there are some fascinating stones with allegorical pictures and some texts written to appear like pictures (it was a Qing fashion to create pictures composed of Chinese characters).

Room Three houses the calligraphy collection which is of great importance. The first stone on the right was carved by Shi Mengying in 999 during the Northern Song dynasty. It shows characters in ancient seal script with, written very small below each of these, the corresponding character in the later regular script. This is of particular interest for those studying the origin and evolution of Chinese characters. There are also two reconstructed examples of the calligraphy of Wang Xizhi (AD 321–379) which have had immense influence on the art of the brush, together with pieces by many of the Tang-dynasty masters.

If you would like to see the famous Nestorian Stele, cut in 781, it is in Room Two, immediately to the left of the entrance. It records the history of the Nestorian Christian community in Chang'an from its founding in the seventh century by a Syrian missionary. Note the tiny cross inscribed at the top and the decorative Arabic script at the bottom. Room One contains the nucleus of the collection, the set of 114 stones engraved in AD 837 with the definitive text of the Confucian classics. Inscribed on both sides of the stones, the text uses a staggering total of 650,252 characters.

Room Five exhibits stone tablets of Song. Yuan, Ming and Qing dynasties. They are mainly concerned with temple renovation and records of merit, although some are also noted for their calligraphic artistic value. In Room Six most of the inscriptions are poetic, inscribed by the literati of the Yuan, Ming and Qing. Emperors, noted ministers and famous calligraphers of various dynasties have left many inscriptions, examples of which are displayed in Room Seven.

THE STONE SCULPTURE GALLERY

This gallery, which is beside the Forest of Steles, has a collection of about 70 sculptures and relief carving of unrivalled quality. It was closed for some time for renovation but was reopened in September 1999. The exhibits are very well presented and stylishly lit, with good captions in English.

The most famous exhibits are the six bas-reliefs from Zhao Ling, the Mausoleum of Emperor Tang Taizong, a great military commander who was particularly fond of horses. The six bas-reliefs of his favourite mounts including his most famous horse,

Quanmo, were originally placed at the northern entrance to the tomb. The Quanmo stone, together with one other, was taken to the United States by an American archaeologist in 1914. They are now in the Art Museum of the University of Pennsylvania. The other four original stones are on display, along with plaster reproductions of the two in America. The originals were sadly broken in several places in 1918, apparently in an attempt to facilitate their transport abroad.

Portrait of Confucius on a stone tablet in the Forest of Steles Museum

A number of large animals which once lined the approaches to imperial tombs of the Han and Tang are also exhibited, including lions, a tiger, a rhinoceros and an ostrich. There is also the inscribed black jade-stone sarcophagus and tomb door of Li Shou, the cousin of first Tang emperor Gaozu, which was unearthed in 1973.

The exhibition also contains several Buddhist statues including a very beautiful torso of a bodhisattva, showing strong Indian influence, and a Avalokitesvara on a elaborate lotus throne. Both are from the Tang period.

Outside the sculpture gallery stands a collection of stone hitching posts, used during the Ming and Qing dynasties for tying up horses. The tops are usually decorated with carved lions. There are two rows of these, one either side of the path, just inside the entrance to the museum.

THE NATIONAL MUSEUM OF SHAANXI HISTORY

The National Museum of Shaanxi History opened in 1991, eighteen years after Premier Zhou Enlai first suggested that such an establishment was needed to exhibit the province's archaeological treasures. Occupying a large site in Xi'an's southern suburbs close to the Big Goose Pagoda, the museum, housed in a complex of striking Tang-dynasty style pavilions, is an absolute must for every visitor to the city.

The exhibits here represent the very best of the museum's collection, the greater portion of which remain stored in its underground warehouse. The permanent exhibition on the ground and first floors is supplemented by touring exhibitions— usually two—in the basement. Included elsewhere in the palatial-style buildings are lecture theatres, conference rooms, a library, research laboratories and an extensive restoration centre. A new unit for restoration has been funded by an Italian Antiquities Department donation of US$4 million.

For security reasons, visitors to the museum must leave their bags in the cloak-room before entering the galleries.

A specious entrance hall greets visitors with its reproduction lion from Shun Ling, the tomb of Wu Zetian's mother. Pace yourself on the stunning marathon walk through a million years of Chinese history. You need about three hours in this museum to do it justice. For longer-stay visitors to Xi'an, a return visit after trips to outlying sites may help to put the sights they have seen into context.

The exhibits on the ground and first floors are arranged in chronological dynastic order.

PREHISTORY TO 2000 BC

At the entrance to the first gallery a relief map of Shaanxi Province shows the three main landscape divisions of the province, from north to south: the loess lands of the

Yellow Earth Plateau, the Guanzhong Plain around the Wei River and the Qinling mountains. Most of the exhibits in this museum were unearthed from the Guanzhong Plain, one of the cradles of Chinese civilization. Relics in this room hail from Shaanxi's three main prehistoric sites—Lantian, Dali and Banpo. Fossilized remains of old Stone-Age man were discovered at Lantian and Dali, while at Banpo the foundations of a Neolithic village have been excavated (see page 42). Pottery with distinctive markings were among the most remarkable finds at Banpo.

XIA, SHANG, WESTERN AND EASTERN ZHOU DYNASTIES

The second gallery covers the 21st century BC to 770 BC, the dawn of the iron and bronze ages. By the Shang and Zhou dynasties, metalworking techniques had become highly sophisticated. Bronze was used in weapons for hunting as well as in battle, ritual implements, agricultural tools, and household and palace utensils. Particularly striking are the handsome cooking tripods called *ding*, some up to one metre (3.3 feet) in height. The Chinese government sent a replica of the largest tripod cooking vessel on display as a gift to the United Nations headquarters. Also look out for the four-legged cooking vessel from the Shang dynasty, which is the only one of its kind. Elegant bulbous-based and thin-legged wine vessels call *jue* were used for warming liquor. Weapons include daggers, halberds and spear-heads, as well as stick-shaped scabbards with sawtooth edges.

Moving onto the relics from the Western Zhou and later the Eastern Zhou, one sees the same material, bronze, cast into more elegant, beautiful and practical wares. Extremely impressive are the bronze bells. There is a single Shicheng Bell, about the size of the largest of watermelons, a musical instrument used in the home of a nobleman or even at court. In a separate display case close-by is one of the museum's finest pieces, a set of chime bells (*bianzhong*). The set consists of eight bells suspended from a wooden beam and arranged according to size. Strangely enough, although their number

A Song-dynasty celadon pot on display in the National Museum of Shaanxi History

corresponds to the eight notes of an octave, the forth and seventh notes, *fa* and *ti*, are absent. Discovered at Fufeng County, the bells were almost certainly used to entertain the courts established by the Zhou (see page 43).

Other examples of aesthetic refinement in Zhou bronzeware include a fine ox-shaped wine vessel, an ornate incense burner and an artist's palette.

SPRING AND AUTUMN PERIOD, THE WARRING STATES AND QIN DYNASTY 770 BC–206 BC

In the third gallery the exhibits highlight progress made during the Qin dynasty in the fields of construction, plumbing, metallurgy, agriculture and irrigation, weaponry and public works. However, rapid economic and technical development had already begun to take place in the pre-imperial period. Around 400 BC, the casting of iron became widespread, as evidenced by the many remains of axes, spades and swords excavated in Shaanxi, a region rich in minerals.

The most important relics from Qin times are, of course, the terracotta warriors (four of which are on display here), but visitors are sure to go to the museum built at the excavations (see page 47). Look instead for a tiger tally. It is quite small, but this ingenious object was a symbol of imperial authority—its holder or recipient could be certain orders were genuine if both halves of the tally matched. Although not immediately apparent, the tally comes in two symmetrical parts split along the animal's backbone.

There is also a very interesting exhibit demonstrating the standardization of weights, measures and coinage that took place at this time.

HAN DYNASTY 202 BC–AD 220

An elaborate wooden map on the wall in this exhibition room, the first one upstairs on the left, highlights the expansion of Han China. The Silk Road became important during this period (see page 63). Travellers who have visited the Han tombs north of Xi'an will see fine examples of funerary objects, such as a gold incense burner discovered at the tomb of the Han general, Huo Qubing (see page 66). Other excavated tombs in the north Guanzhong Plain have yielded tomb figurines which were on a more modest scale than Qin Shihuangdi's terracotta army, but which nevertheless provide much information about daily life at that time.

To keep the deceased content in the afterlife a variety of models in pottery were produced, including water wells, pigsties, barns and domestic animals such as oxen, chicken and dogs. For those who cannot get to Xianyang Museum, a couple of hundred of the miniature terracotta army are shown here.

Finally, there are a number of exhibits to illustrate Han ingenuity. Paper making, one of the four great Chinese inventions—the others were gunpowder, printing and the compass—is generally attributed to the Han Wudi period of 140–87 BC. This early paper was produced from hemp fibre mixed with ramie by a process of pulping, boiling and drying. Another material unique to China was silk—there is an exquisite gilded bronze silkworm from this period which was used as a burial object. A third group of relics includes gear cogs, nuts and hinges.

WEI, JIN, NORTHERN AND SOUTHERN DYNASTIES AD 220–581

A small room is devoted to the relics of this period, during which Chang'an lost its capital status and remained relatively unimportant until it regained its pre-eminence as a centre of imperial power and cultural influence under the Tang rulers.

SUI AND TANG DYNASTY AD 581–907

This was a period that corresponds to Xi'an's restoration as the unified empire's capital. In particular, the brilliance of the mid-Tang period is reflected in the most extensive and spectacular collection of exhibits in this museum. A wooden map, similar to the one in the Han gallery, shows the expansion of Tang China, which capitalized on Sui unification and encompassed present-day Mongolia. Vietnam and parts of Kazakhstan as well as what we recognize as the People's Republic of China today. Beyond, one is confronted by display cases full of markedly colourful relics, consisting in the main of tri-coloured glazed pottery articles. Foremost amongst these are the handsome horses and camels, which bear witness to Chang'an's links to foreign lands by means of the Silk Road. Other figures include heavenly gods stamping on evil and ugly beasts representing ghosts; gargoyle-like animals which were used as guardians of tombs; and Tang beauties with chubby cheeks and bouffant hairstyles, shod in shoes with upturned toes. The vanity of Tang women is highlighted by the mirrors on display. These are of highly polished metal, but it is their ornately decorated backs that are of particular interest.

As a backdrop to these colourful relics, some replicas of murals removed from tomb passageways and chambers are displayed. The themes illustrated relate to recreation, fashion and court activities. Most striking are murals showing polo-playing, hunting, ladies being attended by maidservants and court officials receiving foreign guests. The originals are so delicate and sensitive that they have to be stored in a special climate-controlled room in the museum and are only accessible to very special visitors.

SONG, YUAN, MING AND QING DYNASTIES

Chang'an was eclipsed with the collapse of the Tang in the early tenth century and neither Xi'an nor its environs ever dominated national affairs again. Although spanning a millennium, the relics from this period only occupy a small area.

Particularly noteworthy, however, are the fine porcelain pieces, characteristically sea-green or ivory in colour. There are also some examples of *mi se*, or secret colour, porcelain plates. Pale olive green in colour, this material is so named because even today scientists are unable to replicate the manufacturing process. These particular examples are from the crypt of Famen Temple (see page 105). Another striking display relates to the Ming—an array of 300 colourfully painted miniature pottery figures unearthed at the tomb of a Shaanxi official.

THE BELL TOWER

Each Ming city had a bell tower and a drum tower. The bell was sounded at dawn and the drum at dusk. The two buildings still exist in many Chinese cities, but those at Xi'an are the best known in China.

The Bell Tower was originally built in 1384 at the intersection of Xi Dajie and Guangji Jie. This was the centre of the site of the old Tang Imperial City, where the government offices had been located. The tower was removed in 1582 and rebuilt in its present position in the centre of the southern section of the walled city, overlooking the four avenues which lead to the four gates. It was restored in 1739.

The Bell Tower is set on a square brick platform, each side of which is 35.5 metres (116 feet) long, with an arched gateway at ground level. The platform is 8.6 metres (28 feet) high and on top is a triple-eaved, two-storey wooden structure, a further 27.4 metres (90 feet) high. There is a fine view in all directions from the parapet on the second floor. The inside is remarkable as an example of the very intricate roof truss system used in Ming and Qing wooden architecture. The original great bell no longer exists, but a small replica Ming-period bell is kept in a corner of the brick platform for visitors to strike.

The Bell Tower is open from 8 am to 7 pm. The entrance is via the subway that crosses Bei Dajie.

THE DRUM TOWER

The Drum Tower is quite similar to the nearby Bell Tower, except for its rectangular shape. It was first built in 1380, and restored in 1669, 1739 and 1853. The brick base, on which the wooden structure is built, is 52.6 metres (172 feet) long, 38 metres (125 feet) wide and 7.7 metres (25 feet) high. A road goes straight through it, under a vaulted archway. The triple-roofed, two-storey wooden building is a further 25.3 metres (83 feet) high off its brick platform. The second storey, which is surrounded by a parapet, is now splendidly restored like the Bell Tower, and is used as an antique shop and sometimes holds art exhibitions. The Drum Tower looks down on the irregular grey-tiled roofs of the Muslim quarter.

It is open from 8 am to 7 pm.

THE MING CITY WALL AND GATES

Xi'an's 14th-century wall still stands, although today it is intersected by a few modern roads. It is one of the most important city walls in China and certainly one of the best examples from the Ming.

Construction began during the reign of Hongwu, the first Ming emperor, on the remains of the Sui and Tang wall and took eight years to complete. Repairs and renovation has now been carried out by the local government to restore the wall to its original splendour. The circumference is 13.7 kilometres (8.5 miles), and it is 12 metres (40 feet) high, 12–14 metres (40–46 feet) wide at the top and 15–18 metres (49–59 feet) wide at the bottom. It is surrounded by a moat.

The Ming city gates face the four cardinal points, set off centre in each of the sides of the rectangular wall. Originally each gate had two structures: the gate tower, a triple-eaved building 34.6 metres (114 feet) long, and beyond, on the city wall itself, was the massive archers' tower, 53.2 metres (175 feet) in length, with 48 openings on the outer face from which missiles could be fired on a potential enemy. Visitors are usually taken to the towers above the South Gate, which are well preserved; but instead of guardrooms and barracks you will now find souvenir shops and showrooms inside them.

Reconstructed Ming-dynasty city walls and moat surrounding Xi'an

Access to the top of the wall can also be gained at the North and West Gate, and at all of the smaller gates along the south wall, where landscaping of the area between the wall and moat has provided a pleasant setting for a stroll. It is open from 7 am to 10.30 pm and is attractively lit in the evening, when there are often funfair style attractions on top of the wall near the South Gate.

THE GREAT MOSQUE

The beautiful mosque lies close to the Drum Tower in Huajue Xiang. It is surrounded by the old houses and narrow lanes of Xi'an's Muslim, or Hui, community. The mosque is still active: on ordinary days about 100 men pray there, with perhaps 1,000 on Fridays. Of the ten or so functioning mosques in the city this is the only one which is open to visitors, although non-Muslims are not admitted to the main prayer hall or at prayer times.

Islam has been the most enduring of all faiths in Xi'an. It was first introduced by Arab merchants during the Tang dynasty, and flourished during the Yuan (1279–1368). The Muslims gradually became concentrated in the northwestern part of the walled city, where they remain to this day. The community now numbers about 60,000, one percent of the city's population. There were said to be 14 mosques open before the Cultural Revolution put a stop to Muslim privileges. But today, the community is regaining its lost ground. It has its own primary school, food shops and restaurants (these are popular with the Han Chinese as well). Although the Muslims generally work on Fridays, they do observe Ramadan, the month of fasting from sunrise to sunset. They can often be distinguished from the Han Chinese by their white caps and long beards.

The Great Mosque survived the Cultural Revolution virtually unscathed and remains an outstanding Chinese re-interpretation of an Islamic place of worship. It was founded in AD 742, according to a stone tablet in the mosque, but nothing from this Tang period survives. The present layout dates from the 14th century. Restoration work was done in 1527, 1606 and 1768. The mosque occupies a rectangle 250 metres by 47 metres (820 feet by 155 feet), divided into four courtyards. Throughout there are walls with decoratively carved brick reliefs and the buildings are roofed with beautiful turquoise tiles.

The first courtyard, which was restored in 1981, has an elaborate wooden arch nine metres (29.5 feet) high dating from the 17th century. It contains a stone arch and two free-standing steles. One bears the calligraphy of a famous Song master, Mi Fu (1051–1107), the other that of Dong Qichang of the Ming.

At the entrance to the third courtyard is a Stele Hall with tablets of the Ming and Qing periods inscribed in Chinese, Arabic and Persian. The Stele of the Months, written in Arabic by an imam in 1733, bears information about the Islamic calendar.

In the middle of the third courtyard is the minaret, an octagonal pagoda with a triple roof of turquoise tiles, known as the Shengxin Tower. On either side are sets of rooms. In one section, next to the imam's living quarters, there is a fascinating Qing dynasty map of the Islamic world painted by Chinese Muslims with the black cube of the Kaaba at Mecca in the centre. In the same room is kept an illuminated, hand-written Koran dating from the Qing dynasty.

The fourth courtyard, the principal one of the complex, contains the Prayer Hall. By the entrance is a small room with an upright stele recording in Chinese the foundation of the mosque in AD 742. The stone itself is probably not original. In front of the entrance is the ornamental Phoenix Pavilion with a board proclaiming the 'One Truth of the One God' written during the Ming. Behind the Phoenix Pavilion are two fountains flanked by two small stele pavilions and behind them is the broad, raised stone terrace used for worship.

The large Prayer Hall dates from the Ming: the board outside the main door was bestowed by the Yongle Emperor (reigned 1403–24). The ornate woodwork inside is mainly of this period. There is a coffered ceiling, each panel containing different Arabic inscriptions. The mihrab at the far end has some fine carving.

To walk to the Great Mosque go north along the street that passes under the Drum Tower, and take the first left. A sign in English indicates the way. It is open from 8.30 am to 6 pm.

THE TEMPLE OF THE EIGHT IMMORTALS

China's indigenous religion, Daoism, is best represented in Xi'an by the Temple of the Eight Immortals (Baxian An).

Located just east of the city wall, outside Zhongshan Gate, it housed 100 priests as recently as 20 years ago. But at the start of the Cultural Revolution in 1966 half the buildings were demolished by iconoclastic Red Guards, and those that survived were converted into a machine plant. Under a decade-long restoration programme initiated in 1981, the plant was moved out and the temple halls rebuilt and redecorated.

The temple is now functioning again as a place of worship and a centre for the training of priests. There are now more than 40 of them, easily distinguishable from other Chinese by their long hair, usually plaited and stuffed into one of nine different types of black hat according to their sect, sage-like long beards, white shirts, blue smocks, white gaiters and black canvas shoes.

Although no foundation steles exists, it is thought the temple was established during the Northern Song (AD 960–1127). It expanded during the Yuan and Ming, and became particularly important during the Qing. When the imperial court was in exile in Xi'an (1900–01), the empress Dowager Cixi grew especially fond of the temple and used to go there to paint peonies.

CHIMERA

*T*o this Tang capital, already old in refinement, Arabs and Persian arrived by the Silk Route or the southern ports. They came as merchants and mercenary soldiers, and the houses of their Muslim descendants, who call themselves Hui, still cluster in whitewashed lanes. Yet the people looked identical to Han Chinese, and when I ventured into the chief mosque I was surrounded by pagodas, dragon-screens and tilted eaves. Only when I looked closer did I notice that on some memorials Chinese characters gave way to the dotted swing of Arabic, and the prayer-hall enclosed no plump idol but an empty space, inviting a god only in the mind.

Outside, a few caretakers were sweeping leaves along the garden pathways. The chanting of the Koran sounded from a closed room. In one arcade an old man, the skin peeled white about his eyes, was singing in a high, weak voice, while a quorum of ancients seated round him quavered applause. Amongst them the imam of the mosque—a dark, lordly figure—exuded urbane authority. I sidled into talk with him. I was intrigued, I said, by the provenance of his people.

'We arrived in Xi'an as simple traders', he said, 'and nobody has any record of his ancestry except in his head. Our people came along the Silk Road during the Tang years.' His fingers made a little galloping motion in the air. 'But we stopped speaking Arabic long ago. Even I can only read the classical language of the Koran.'

'But you've been to Mecca?'

'I made the pilgrimage in 1956.'

He was dressed portentously in white cap and blue-grey robes. I played with the idea of his Arab-Persian descent for a while, studying his hirsute chin and tufted eyebrows. But nothing in his face—nor in that of anyone else—betrayed a trace of western Asia. 'You all look Chinese,' I said.

'Yes,' he answered bluntly. 'I can't tell any difference myself, not in any of us—and there are fifty thousand Hui in the city. But I suppose if we hadn't intermarried we would have died out. Still, it's a mystery.'

'In the Cultural Revolution...'

'Oh that.' He smoothed his hands resolutely over his robes. 'The Red Guards arrived planning to smash up the mosque, but I sat them down and talked to them. I told them this was a historical place of great importance. Then...'—even now he looked surprised by the outcome—'then they just left. They simply went away.' A flicker of his fingers dispelled them. 'The mosque was closed down, of course, and we went into the fields... But nobody touched it.'

A lesser man would have called it a miracle.

Colin Thubron, Behind the Wall

Xi'an Muslims at prayer

THE XI'AN INCIDENT

Xi'an has always been known to the Chinese as a city rich with history, but it only gained recognition in much of the Western world in 1936 when Generalissimo Chiang Kai-shek was kidnapped there by some of his own generals.

The Xi'an Incident, as it became known, held the leadership of China hanging in the balance for a couple of tension-wracked weeks. An intriguing sequence of events brought on the kidnapping and its solution.

In 1936, while Hitler marched in Europe, the Japanese army was steadily tightening its grip on China. Chiang Kai-shek was not so much in control as simply being at the top of a fragile coalition of Chinese warlords and armies spread over China. The communists had escaped Chiang's pursuit on the Long March and established themselves securely at Yan'an, in the mountains north of Xi'an.

Chiang knew that a head-on conflict with the Japanese army would, if not demolish him, at least weaken his position, and make him vulnerable to the communists. He decided to appease the Japanese instead, and send many of his troops to fight the communists.

But for Zhang Xueliang, one of Chiang's allied generals, this policy of foot-dragging against the Japanese was unacceptable. A bright and courageous young general, Zhang was head of a Manchurian army and was incensed at the way his home in northeast China had been overrun by the Japanese since 1931. Zhang saw the situation deteriorating further in 1936, when the Japanese made a dramatic attack into Suiyan, a key area north of Beijing. On 4 December, a Nationalist attack on the communists failed, resulting in a widespread refusal amongst Chiang's troops to continue fighting. Chiang flew to Xi'an to direct the campaign himself.

Zhang saw this as an ideal moment to make a move. He discreetly made contact with the communists and at dawn on 12 December, his troops surrounded the palace at Huaqing Hot Springs, where Chiang was quartered. Hearing gunfire, Chiang escaped barefoot in his nightshirt—leaving his dentures behind—scaled a wall, injuring his back, and scurried up an old path on Black Horse Mountain. Thirty of his men were killed defending him.

Zhang's officers combed the area, and one of them found their Generalissimo later that afternoon, shivering and in pain, crouched in a crevice between the rocks. As the officer moved to bind Chiang's hands, the Generalissimo reminded his captor that he was the Commander-in-Chief. The officer is said to have bowed politely to Chiang and replied, 'You are also our prisoner.'

Two weeks of tough negotiations followed. Chiang and his formidable wife, Soong May-ling, were on one side, with Zhang and Zhou Enlai, later communist China's Premier, on the other, while the rest of China waited impatiently. Many of the communist leaders wanted to execute Chiang, or at least keep him imprisoned. But a cable arrived from Moscow with an order from Stalin to release Chiang and get on with the task of fighting the Japanese.

The Chinese communists bristled at being told by 'Uncle Joe' how to handle what they saw as their own affair. But they also knew they could win some useful concessions out of Chiang if they released him.

In the end, a compromise was reached. Chiang was allowed to fly back to Nanjing a free man, but had to give up the pretence of being the sole leader of China. Ostensibly he joined with the communists in a 'National Front' against the Japanese. Zhang Xueliang, who also went back to Nanjing, was a hero only temporarily and was soon arrested by Chiang and branded a traitor.

The visitor to Huaqing Hot Springs can still see the site of this famous incident. The rooms where Chiang stayed and worked are marked, as is the spot up the hill where the Generalissimo was actually caught. The hiding place is marked by a chain and nearby, commemorating the capture, is a pavilion of dignified Grecian structure.

LOST LUGGAGE IN SIANFU

In June 1936, the American correspondent Edgar Snow left the peaceful campus of Yanjing University in Beijing, where he had been teaching in the school of journalism, to travel to the war-torn hinterland of China on his toughest mission to date. Five years previously the Japanese had annexed Manchuria. Further incursions by the Japanese went unchecked as civil war between Nationalists and communists kept the armies occupied. Just eight months before, Mao Zedong had led the communist retreat—later called the Long March—from soviet areas in the southeastern province of Jiangxi to a new base in northern Shaanxi. Edgar Snow wanted to find the Red Bandits, as the communists were called, interview their leader Mao, and report their manifesto for China to the world.

Inoculated against smallpox, cholera, typhus, plague and typhoid and armed with a letter written in invisible ink testifying his credentials as a trustworthy journalist, Snow boarded the night train to Zhengzhou where he would change for Sianfu (present-day Xi'an). Later he disclosed that the introduction was written by Soong Chingling, widow of Sun Yat-sen.

Sianfu—Prefecture of Western Peace—was the headquarters of two warlords and their own troops: General Yang Hucheng and Marshall Zhang Xueliang. Both were poised to implement what Generalissimo Chiang Kai-shek hoped would be the final suppression of the Red Bandits in the north.

On arrival at Sianfu's 'new and handsome railway station', Edgar Snow took a room, as he had been instructed, in the Xijing Hotel on the west side of present-day Jiefang Lu (the building now houses the Provincial Travel Bureau). There he waited patiently for a man who would identify himself as 'Wang'. A few days later, a pastor of that name, fluent in English thanks to his missionary education in Shanghai, came to the hotel. He was to be the go-between responsible for arranging Snow's onward travel to the communists' capital of Bao'an, 350 kilometres (217 miles) away in the north.

A few day later Snow, escorted by troops from Zhang Xueliang's army, passed through the high wooden gates of the walled city in the half light of dawn. After crossing the Wei River by ferry and passing through a strip of no man's land, he reached Red territory. From a village within this territory, where he met Zhou Enlai, he was escorted at last into the presence of the communist leader.

What happened in the ensuing few months is journalistic history. Snow interviewed Mao Zedong over many nights, taking notes which in the end totalled about 20,000 words. From these and talks with other leaders Snow was able to write the first authentic account of the life and conditions of the northwestern communist enclave, the revolutionary struggles of Mao and his comrades, and the fundamental policies of the People's Soviet Republic.

In mid-October 1936, Snow bid farewell to his communist hosts, and about a week later crossed safely behind Nationalist lines again. He rode on to a town where a truck waited to take him back to Sianfu. As he prepared to disembark near the Drum Tower, he asked one of his escorts to toss down his kitbag. To his horror, it could not be found. In the bag were a dozen diaries and notebooks, 30 rolls of film and many magazines, newspapers and documents he had collected during his time in Red territory. It then dawned on the travellers that Snow's bag had been stuffed into a gunnysack amongst broken rifles and guns, which had been offloaded at Xianyang 30 kilometres (18 miles) back.

The truck driver proposed they waited till the next day to retrieve the bag, but Snow insisted on the search being made without delay. The driver returned to Xianyang and the precious bag was recovered. Snow's sense of urgency proved justified. The next day much of Sianfu was cordoned off and traffic was cleared from the roads, for Chiang Kai-shek had decided to pay a sudden call on the city.

The manuscript of *Red Star over China* was completed within an astonishing eight months in Beijing, where Snow returned to live. The 500-page epic was first published in England in 1937 and has since become a classic.

In Xi'an, Edgar Snow's contribution to the world's understanding of Chinese communism is remembered by the Snow Studies Centre, based at the Eighth Route Army Office Museum (see page ???). The centre was established in February 1992, the 20th anniversary of Snow's death. Many of the journalist's belongings, including his khaki uniform, knapsack and grass sandals, were donated to the centre by his family.

THE TEMPLE OF THE TOWN GOD

Within walking distance of the Bell Tower, this temple is now occupied by the bustling Town God Temple Market (Chenghuang Miao). Walk west from the Bell Tower along Xi Dajie and look for the entrance on the right, set back from the road. Walking through a busy arcade of stalls selling all kinds of bric-a-brac and household items, one is amongst the temple buildings before realizing it. Some of the buildings are even used as storerooms or shops. Considering it has not been maintained it is in surprisingly good condition although much of the paint on the woodwork has disappeared.

The temple dates back to 1389, but was moved to its present site in 1432. It has been rebuilt and restored many times since, notably in 1723 when materials were utilized from the 14th-century palace of the Prince of Qin, Zhu Shuang. The main hall, built in 1723, survives with ornate carved doors and a roof of turquoise glazed tiles. In front of it there is an elaborate wooden arch in good condition.

REVOLUTION PARK

Revolution Park (Geming Gongyuan), in the northeast of the walled city, is where those who died in the 1926 Siege of Xi'an are buried. Anti-Nationalist forces laid siege to Xi'an on 15 May 1926 after the city had been occupied by a pro-Nationalist general, Yang Hucheng. Despite appalling starvation and a fierce bombing attack, the city held out until 28 November 1926, when the siege was finally lifted. Yang Hucheng wrote the funeral couplet for those 50,000 inhabitants and refugees who are said to have died during the siege:

> They led glorious lives and died a glorious death.
> Their merits are known throughout Shaanxi, as are their regrets.

The park contains a three-storey pagoda erected in 1927, and is very popular with the locals, especially on Sundays.

THE EIGHTH ROUTE ARMY OFFICE MUSEUM

Near Revolution Park at 1 Qixianzhuang, just off Beixin Jie, is the Eighth Route Army Office (initially called the Red Army Liaison Office) which is now a museum. It was founded immediately after the Xi'an incident which had resulted in the Nationalists and communists joining forces against the Japanese (see page 130).

The office once linked the headquarters of the Communist Party in Yan'an in northern Shaanxi with the outside world in the struggle against the Japanese. It obtained vital supplies for Yan'an, helped recruits make their way there, and publicized the polices of the party leadership. The office functioned until 10 September 1946. It is now preserved as it was during the Sino-Japanese War.

Occupying a series of plain, grey and white one-storey buildings set around four courtyards, the museum is a good deal more interesting than its name might suggest. There is an exhibition room with many fascinating photographs taken in Shaanxi during the 1930s and '40s. Visitors are also shown where important communist leaders, including Zhou Enlai, Deng Xiaoping, Zhu De and Liu Shaoqi stayed. The rooms are small and spartan with little more than a table, chair and a bed. The Canadian doctor Norman Bethune, later to become almost a cult figure in China, was also once a visitor here. The museum houses the Snow Studies Centre (see page 132), which was opened in 1992.

The office still has its 1939 Chevrolet, originally imported from Hong Kong and used for urgent missions to Yan'an. The radio room contains the old transmitter and receiver, and the well they had to draw their bitter water from still exists. Even the director of the museum is an interesting character: Tang Bin, a veteran soldier, joined the Communist Fourth Route Army in Sichuan in 1933, when he was only 16, and eventually became a guard in the Eighth Route Army Office in Lanzhou from 1938 to 1946, later rising to a company commander in the air force.

The museum is open 9 am to 5 pm.

QIN PALACE FILM SET

This reproduction Qin Palace, a few minutes walk east of the Big Goose Pagoda, was built in 1988 for the IMAX film *Qin Shihuang*, a joint-venture production between Xi'an film Studio and the Canadian State Film Bureau.

According to legend, the First Emperor, Qin Shihuangdi, used the weapons he confiscated to make 12 monolithic copper statues. Replicas of these stand sentinel on the avenue approach to the palace. Climbing up the long flight of steps you reach the only hall of the palace, where dummies are dressed in Qin costume. The climb is worth the effort if only to stand and admire the view and imagine for a moment you are the emperor looking down on the giant statues.

On the right hand side of the hall is an exhibition room displaying stills of Xi'an Film Studio's most successful movies, notably *Life*, *Red Sorghum* (filmed in Shandong), and more recently *After the Final Battle*, a look at the re-education of Kuomintang officers in the post-Liberation years of the people's Republic.

A large dusty concourse in front of the elevated palace façade is dotted with a hotchpotch of redundant film-set props, including tanks, concrete horses and chariots.

Just inside the entrance to the left is a mock Qin-dynasty street lined with shops used during the filming, however, these now sell tourist souvenirs. Just around the corner on the left look for the young lady shop assistant who spends her spare time playing the Guzheng, a classical Chinese stringed instrument. She is quite good and if you can persuade her to give a short recital it will be worth the price of the admission.

THE PEASANT PAINTERS OF HUXIAN

In 1958, a group of farmers in Huxian, a county some 40 kilometres (25 miles) outside Xi'an, did some paintings to record progress on the construction of a new reservoir. So successful were the works that they inspired the organization of special painting centres to help the peasants develop their art. By the mid-1970s, there were about 2,000 active painters in the county, all of them farmers who would bicycle to the centres after a hard day's work in the fields. These centres are still the support system of Huxian's peasant artists. Painting materials and a certain amount of professional guidance are given, but the basic technical tuition does not seem to have stifled the creative independence of the better painters of the Huxian group.

The distinctive style developed by the Huxian painters has won them national, and international, recognition. Exhibitions have already been

held in Hong Kong, Sweden, London, the US and Canada, as well as in Beijing and Shanghai.

The paintings are a complete contrast from the misty landscapes and muted colours of classic Chinese watercolours. The work of the peasants of Huxian is humorous, vibrant, dependent on brilliant colour and intricate surface pattern, sometimes with a total disregard for perspective. A hint of the intricate design of local embroidery is carried through to the paintings.

Themes chosen reflect the painter's everyday life as farmers—drying fish, feeding chickens, reeling silk, wedding parties and other festivities.

Some painters record, with an almost childlike accuracy of observation, change within their society—horses hauling carts of concrete, for example, or a confrontation between an ox-drawn cart and a tractor. Legend and traditional opera stories are also a rich source of themes for the painters.

The group claims that over 100,000 paintings have already been produced. Visitors to Xi'an will find paintings on sale at most sightseeing spots, but top quality work from the most creative artists of the group is more difficult to come by, and more expensive. The work of Wang Jinglong, which is strikingly different from most of the group, has already aroused worldwide interest on account of its distinctive individual interpretation of everyday happenings. Luo Zhijin and Liu Fengtao are two other names to look out for.

Apart from the exhibition hall at Huxian itself, good selection of paintings can be found in Xi'an at the Little Goose Pagoda and at the Tang Dynasty Art Museum. The latter has originals for sale by Cheng Minsheng and the female artist Pan Xiaoling, whose work has been exhibited in New York.

Family plots in the Countryside (left), and Pulling Concrete (above); Huxian paintings by Wang Jinglong

WEAVING A SPELL

*H*ere *was a kaleidoscope of colour beyond belief within a dusty desert place, as refreshingly different as discovering Van Gogh's 'Sunflowers' amongst the murky Manchester factories and figures of Lowry. A sword is brandished above a trailing satin sleeve, the fiery orange of dancing flames. Yellow silk of Sun and Earth is the Emperor's colour, embroidered with a red-tongued golden dragon. Mood is swiftly changed as these vivid silken robes shimmer in the hot caressing breeze, suddenly enlivened by the dramatic overtures of a white-bearded man toward a timid young maiden, as he rushed shrieking to left, to right. The musicians, accommodated at the side of the cast-concrete stage, produce a mixture of melody and sound-effects to fit the action, emotion and body language. The conflict of a sword is created by a rapid and voluminous thrashing of drum and cymbal; remorse and contemplation by the sad drone of the two-stringed erhu; gaiety by the bird-like chatter of the dizi bamboo flute; and tranquillity by the subtle plucking of the moon guitar. Exits are made to a flurried finale of everything that the orchestra can muster.*

Backstage is the open-air dressing, make-up and green room rolled into one. The trunks of this travelling troupe lay open, overflowing with the finest embroidered silks. Masks, beards, bald heads and head-dresses lie strewn in apparent confusion. Oblivious to the crowd of peasants a young girl makes up as the Empress. She picks up colour from a tiny paintbox, guiding herself with the use of a palm-sized mirror. She pales her oriental complexion to eggshell smoothness. Her slender tapering eyes are accentuated. She pouts her lips to paint on their apex a slim scarlet rosebud, and rouges her cheeks to the subtle tint of a ripening apple. Only then does this girl allow her face to be dimpled by a smile of majestic beauty. Crowned with a head-dress of red silk and silver she enters the stage, followed by ladies of the court to a deafening fanfare.

William Lindesay, Alone on the Great Wall

Recommended Reading

HISTORY AND RELIGION

K Ch'en: *Buddhism in China, Historical Survey* (Princeton University Press, Princetown, New Jersey, 1964)

J Bertram: *First Act in China: The Story of the Sian Mutiny* (1938, reprinted by Hyperion Press, Westport, Conn, 1973)

M Zanchen (translated by Wang Zhao): *The Life of General Yang Hucheng* (Joint Publishing Company, Hong Kong 1981)

E Reischauer: *Ennin's Dairy* (Ronald Press Company, New York, 1955)

Peter Hopkirk: *Foreign Devils on the Silk Road* (Oxford University Press reprint, 1986)

Edgar Snow: *Red Star Over China* (Random House, USA, 1938)

ARTS AND ARCHAEOLOGY

W Watson: *Ancient China, The Discoveries of Post-Liberation Archaeology* (BBC, London, 1974)

B Laufer: *Chinese Pottery of the Han Dynasty* (1909, reprinted by Charles E Tuttle, Vermont and Tokyo, 1962)

The Subterranean Army of Emperor Qin Shi Huang (China Travel and Tourism Press, 1999)

Xi'an: World Ancient Chinese Capital for over a Thousand Years (Shaanxi People's Fine Arts Publishing House, 1990)

Li Hui: *Xi'an: The Famous Ancient Capital of China* (Shaanxi Tourism Bureau, 1990)

The Pick of Prehistoric Cultural Relics of Ban Po Museum (Shaanxi Tourism Publishing House, 1995)

Wang Xueli: *The Coloured Figurines in Yang Ling Mausoleum of Han in China* (China Shaanxi Travel and Tourism Press, 1992)

LITERATURE

Arthur Cooper: *Li Po and Tu Fu* (Penguin Books, Harmondsworth, 1979)

Y Inoue (translated by J T Araki and E Seidensticker): *Lou-lan and Other Stories* (Kodansha International Limited, New York and San Francisco, 1979)

E R Hughes: *Two Chinese Poets, Vignettes of Han Life and Thought* (Princeton University Press, Princeton, New Jersey, 1960)

Arthur Waley: *The Life and Times of Po Chü-i 772–846* (George Allen & Unwin, London, 1949)

Translated by Yang Xianyi and Gladys Yang: *Poetry and Prose of the Tang and Song* (Panda Books, Beijing, 1984)

TWENTIETH-CENTURY TRAVELLERS

Violet Cressy-Marcks: *Journey into China* (Hodder and Stoughton, London, 1940)

S Eliasson (translated by K John): *Dragon Wang's River* (Methuen and Company Limited, London, 1957)

R Farrar: *On the Eaves of the World* (E Arnold, London, 1917)

Peter Fleming: *News Form Tartary* (1936, reprinted by Futura Publications, London, 1980)

F H Nichols: *Through Hidden Shensi* (Charles Scribner's Sons, New York, 1902)

R Stirling Clark and A de C Sowerby: *Through Shen-Kan: The Account of the Clark Expedition in North China 1908–09* (T Fisher Unwin, London, 1912)

Lynn Pan: *China's Sorrow—Journeys Around the Yellow River* (Century, London, 1985)

William Lindesay: *Alone on the Great Wall* (Hodder & Stoughton, London, 1989 and Fulcrum Publishing, Colorado, USA, 1991)

Shaanxi farmers normally have little time for relaxation, producing as they do, two main crops per year in their fields—one of maize and the other of winter wheat—together with chillies and fruit, including pomegranates, persimmons, apples and pears

A GUIDE TO PRONOUNCING CHINESE NAMES

The official system of Romanization used in China, which the visitor will find on maps, road signs and city shopfronts, is known as *Pinyin*. It is now almost universally adopted by the Western media.

Some visitors may initially encounter some difficulty in pronouncing Romanized Chinese words. In fact many of the sounds correspond to the usual pronunciation of the letters in English. The exceptions are:

Initials

c	is like the *ts* in 'i*ts*'
q	is like the *ch* in '*cheese*'
x	has no English equivalent, and can best be described as a hissing consonant that lies somewhere between *sh* and *s*. The sound was rendered as *hs* under an earlier transcription system.
z	is like the *ds* in 'fa*ds*'
zh	is unaspirated, and sounds like the *j* in 'jug'.

Finals

a	sounds like '*ah*'
e	is pronounced as in 'h*er*'
i	is pronounced as in 'sk*i*' (written as y*i* when not preceded by an initial consonant). However, in *ci*, *chi*, *ri*, *shi*, *zi* and *zhi*, the sound represented by the final is quite different and is similar to the *ir* in 'sir' but without much stressing of the *r* sound.
o	sounds like the *aw* in 'l*aw*'
u	sounds like the *oo* in '*ooze*'
ü	is pronounced as the German *ü* (written as y*u* when not preceded by an initial consonant). The *ê* and *ü* are usually written simply as *e* and *u*.

Finals in Combination

When two or more finals are combined, such as in *hao*, *jiao* and *liu*, each letter retains its sound value as indicated in the list above, but note the following:

ai	is like the *ie* in 'tie'
ei	is like the *ay* in 'bay'
ian	is like the *ien* in 'Vienna'
ie	similar to 'ear'
ou	is like the *o* in 'code'
uai	sounds like 'why'
uan	is like the *uan* in 'iguana'
	(except when proceeded by *j, q, x* and *y*; in these cases a *u* following any of these four consonants is in fact *ü* and *uan* is similar to *uen*.)
ue	is like the *ue* in 'duet'
ui	sounds like 'way'

Examples

A few Chinese names are shown below with English phonetic spelling beside them:

Beijing	Bay-jing
Cixi	Tsi-shee
Guilin	Gway-lin
Hangzhou	Hahng-joe
Kangxi	Kahng-shee
Qianlong	Chien-loong
Tiantai	Tien-tie
Xian	Shee-ahn

An apostrophe is used to separate syllables in certain compound-character words to preclude confusion. For example, *Changan* (which can be *chang-an* or *chan-gan*) is sometimes written as *Chang'an*.

Tones

A Chinese syllable consists of not only an initial and a final or finals, but also a tone or pitch of the voice when the words are spoken. In *Pinyin* the four basic tones are marked ˉ , ´ , ˇ and ` . These marks are almost never shown in printed form except in language texts.

A CHRONOLOGY OF PERIODS IN CHINESE HISTORY

Palaeolithic	c.600,000–7000 BC
Neolithic	c.7000–1600 BC
Shang	c.1600–1027 BC
Western Zhou	1027–771 BC
Eastern Zhou	770–256 BC
Spring and Autumn Annals	770–476 BC
Warring States	475–221 BC
Qin	221–206 BC
Western (Former) Han	206 BC–8 AD
Xin	9–24
Eastern (Later) Han	25–220
Three Kingdoms	220–265
Western Jin	265–316
Northern and Southern Dynasties	317–589
Sixteen Kingdoms	317–439
Former Zhao	304–329
Former Qin	351–383
Later Qin	384–417
Northern Wei	386–534
Western Wei	535–556
Northern Zhou	557–581
Sui	581–618
Tang	618–907
Five Dynasties	907–960
Northern Song	960–1127
Southern Song	1127–1279
Jin (Jurchen)	1115–1234
Yuan (Mongol)	1279–1368
Ming	1368–1644
Qing (Manchu)	1644–1911
Republic of China	1911–1949
People's Republic of China	1949–

One of the massive stone guardians that line the 'Spirit Way' of Qian Ling, the mausoleum of Tang emperor Gaozong and his empress Wu Zetian

Practical Information

Hotels

Xi'an did not have a Western-style hotel until the 1950s. In the early part of the century Chinese inns were open to foreigners, but many Western travellers arriving in Xi'an stayed with the European missionaries of the Scandinavian Alliance, the English Baptist Mission and the China Inland Mission.

Since the city's first joint-venture hotel, the Golden Flower, opened in 1985, many new international-standard hotels have been built. Now Xi'an has a surplus of quality accommodation, so that even in the peak seasons of spring and autumn many hotels still have a large percentage of their rooms vacant. In the winter, from mid-November until the end of March, these hotels offer various bargain packages whereby tariffs are reduced, sometimes by up to 50 per cent. Check with individual hotels directly.

Shangri-La Golden Flower Hotel (Xiang Ge Li La Jinhua Fandian)
8 Changle Xilu. Tel. (029) 3232981; fax. (029) 3232888; e-mail: slx@shangri-la.com
香格里拉金花饭店 长乐西路 8 号
Five-star hotel situated outside the city wall on the road to the Terracotta Warriors. 446 of the largest rooms in Xi'an, and the largest swimming pool. Recently completed a US$3.5 million renovation project. Restaurants serving Cantonese, Shaanxi and international cuisine (see Restaurant section on page 150).

Hyatt Hotel (Kaiyue Fandian)
158 Dong Dajie. Tel. (029) 7231234; fax. (029) 7216799
凯悦饭店 东大街 158 号
Situated within the city walls and close to the business and shopping districts. 404 luxurious rooms. Various restaurants serving both international and Chinese cuisine, pub and pizzeria. Business centre, health club, beauty salon and shopping facilities.

Sheraton Xi'an Hotel (Xi'an Xi Lai Deng Jiudian)
12 Fenghao Lu. Tel. (029) 4261888; fax. (029) 4262983; website: http://www.sheraton.com
西安喜来登酒店 丰镐路 12 号
Five-star hotel conveniently located to the west of the city wall. 438 luxuriously equipped rooms.

ANA Grand Castle Hotel (Chang'an Chengbao Da Jiudian)
12 Huancheng Nanlu Xiduan. Tel. (029) 7231800; fax. (029) 7231500; e-mail: anasales@pub.xaonline.com
长安城堡大酒店 环城南路西段 12 号

Modern five-star hotel conveniently located facing the south gate of the city wall. 340 rooms and suites. Spacious atrium lobby lounge, Sky Lounge, Chinese and Japanese restaurants, banqueting hall and coffee shop. Business centre, beauty salon and shopping centre.

Diamond Hotel (Da Er Man Jiudian)
19 Jiangong Lu. Tel. (029) 2229888; fax. (029) 2220888; e-mail: diahtl@pub.xaonline.com
达尔曼大酒店　建工路 19 号
The tallest and newest five-star hotel in Xi'an. Located 15 minutes east of the city wall, this 30-storey hotel features 307 well-appointed rooms and suites, including penthouse and executive suites. Restaurants serving Chinese, Japanese and international cuisine, banqueting and boardroom facilities, bars, nightclub, fully-equipped gymnasium, swimming pool, sauna and massage centre, beauty salon and fully-equipped business centre.

Dynasty Hotel (Qindu Jiudian)
55 Huancheng Xilu. Tel. (029) 8626262; fax. (029) 8627728; e-mail: dynasty@pub.xaonline.com
秦都酒店　环城西路北段 55 号
Conveniently located alongside the west city wall. Modern facilities in ancient Chinese palatial style architecture with 200 rooms. Restaurants and 300-seat banquet room offering hot-pot, Cantonese, Shanghainese, and Western cuisine. Meeting rooms and business centre, sauna and fitness room, beauty salon, bar and nightclub, shopping arcade. Air-ticketing service.

Grand New World Hotel (Gudu Xin Shijie Jiudian)
48 Lianhu Lu. Tel. (029) 7216868; fax. (029) 7210708/7317043; e-mail: gnwhbc@pub.xaonline.com
古都新世界大酒店　莲湖路 48 号
Conveniently located within the walled city. 493 rooms. Fully equipped meeting facilities with 1130 seat theatre and 12 meeting rooms. Four restaurants serving local, Cantonese, continental, American and southeast Asian specialities. Indoor swimming pool, open tennis court, sauna and gymnasium.

Hotel Royal Xi'an (Xi'an Huangcheng Binguan)
334 Dong Dajie. Tel. (029) 7235311; fax. (029) 7235887; e-mail: royalxa@xa.col.com.cn
西安皇城宾官　东大街 334 号
Four-star hotel located within the city walls, managed by Nikko Hotel International. 439 rooms, including two royal suites, and business and deluxe suites. Chinese and Western restaurants, banquet halls, tea lounge, bar. Business centre.

Xi'an Garden Hotel (Xi'an Tanghua Binguan)
4 Yan Yin Lu, Dayan Ta. Tel. (029) 5261111; fax. (029) 5261778/5261998; e-mail:
tanghua@pub.xaonline.com
西安唐华宾官　大雁塔雁引路 4 号
Four-star joint-venture hotel located adjacent to the Big Goose Pagoda in spacious garden
setting. 292 rooms. Chinese, Japanese and Western restaurants. Tang Theatre Restaurant
serving French cuisine also equipped as a conference hall. Sauna, fitness centre and
massage facilities.

Bell Tower Hotel (Zhonglou Fandian)
Southwest corner of Bell Tower. Tel. (029) 7279200; fax. (029) 7218767; e-mail:
bth@sein.sxgr.com.cn
钟楼饭店　钟楼西南角
Good central location overlooking the Bell Tower and a short walk from the Drum Tower
and Great Mosque. 321 fully appointed rooms. Chinese and Western restaurants,
meeting and banquet rooms.

Jianguo Hotel (Jianguo Fandian)
20 Jinhua Nanlu. Tel. (029) 3238888; fax. (029) 3237180/3235145; e-mail:
jgsale@pub.xaonline.com
建国饭店　金花南路 20 号
Located just east of the city wall, near the zoo. Its 800 rooms are equipped with satellite
TV. Banquet hall, conference rooms, a variety of restaurants, swimming pool, sauna,
beauty salon, gym and bicycle rental.

Le Garden Hotel (Li Yuan Jiudian)
8 Lao Dong Nanlu. Tel. (029) 4263388; fax. (029) 4263288; e-mail: xlg@xa.col.com.cn
骊苑酒店　劳动南路 8 号
Four-star hotel located on the ring road to the southeast of the walled city. 298 rooms with
executive and non-smoking floors and meeting rooms. Two Chinese restaurants serving
Cantonese and southeastern cuisine, a Western-style coffee shop, bar and disco. Health
club with gymnasium, sauna, steam bath and jacuzzis, and beauty salon.

Xi'an Hotel (Xi'an Binguan)
36 Chang'an Lu. Tel. (029) 5261351; fax. (029) 5261796
西安宾官　长安路北段 36 号
Four-star, 545-room hotel located close to the Little Goose Pagoda south of the city wall.
Restaurants serve Chinese, Japanese and Western cuisine. Health and recreation centre
including swimming pool and gymnasium. Business centre.

Tangcheng Hotel (Tangcheng Binguan)
3 Hanguan Nanlu. Tel. (029) 5265711; fax. (029) 5261041; e-mail: csxtch@public.xa.sn.cn
唐城宾馆 含光路南段 3 号
Modern three-star hotel, located south of the walled city. 406 rooms and suites, conference rooms, business centre, Chinese and Western restaurants, bars, coffee shop and recreational facilities.

Wannian Hotel (Wannian Fandian)
11 Changle Zhonglu. Tel. (029) 3231932; fax. (029) 3235460; e-mail: wannianhotel@ihw.com.cn
万年饭店 长乐中路 11 号
Located outside the city wall on the road to the Terracotta Warriors. 170 fully appointed rooms. Chinese and international restaurant, lounge bar, health centre, sauna, massage parlour and beauty salon.

Empress Hotel (Huanghou Jiudian)
45 Xingqing Lu. Tel. (029) 3232999; fax. (029) 3236988
皇后酒店 兴庆路 45 号
Located east of the walled city not far from the zoo. 259 spacious rooms. Comprehensive business, entertainment and dining facilities.

City Hotel (Chengshi Jiudian)
70 Nan Dajie. Tel. (029) 7219988; fax. (029) 7216688
城市酒店 南大街 70 号
Located in the city centre just south of the Bell Tower. 138 fully appointed rooms. Chinese and Western restaurants, business centre, beauty salon and air-ticketing service.

Longhai Hotel (Longhai Jiudian)
306 Jiefang Lu. Tel. (029) 7416090; fax. (029) 7416580
陇海大酒店 解放路 306 号
International standard three-star hotel, located in the northeast of the walled city, not far from the railway station. 308 rooms.

Huaqing Guesthouse (Huaqing Chi Binguan)
Lintong County. Tel. (029) 3812002
华清池宾馆 临潼县
Part of the hot springs complex, with 23 rooms. On the road to the Terracotta Army Museum.

XIANYANG

Imperial Hotel (Qinbao Binguan)
60A Weiyang Xilu. Tel. (0910) 3313388; fax. (0910) 3313366; e-mail: qingbao@public.xa.sn.cn
秦宝宾馆　渭阳西路 60A 号
Located in the centre of Xianyang, 15 minutes drive from the international airport. 220 rooms,
conference rooms, Chinese and Western restaurant, coffee shop and business centre.

FAMEN

Famen Temple Hotel (Famen Si Binguan)
Chongzheng Lu. Tel. (0917) 5254141; fax. (0917) 5254273
法门寺宾馆　崇正路
A small but new 36-room hotel close to the Famen Temple.

Restaurants

Golden Flower Hotel Restaurants (Shangri-La Hotel)
8 Changle Xilu. Tel. (029) 3232981
香格里拉金花饭店　长乐西路 8 号
The **Shang Palace** is regarded by the most critical of locals as one of the best restaurants
in the city. The menu features Sichuanese and Cantonese home-style cooking. Some
items on the menu are available only in season. Particularly recommended is the Sichuan
roast duck, a variation of the more famous Beijing counterpart. **Coffee Garden** is a coffee
shop serving international cuisine. The **Lobby Lounge** serves afternoon tea and cocktails
with live musical entertainment. In addition, **Drunken Moon** is an outdoor patio
barbeque-style restaurant which operates during summer and autumn seasons.
Q Bar serves a choice of light snacks and drinks from a 'pub menu'.

The Tang Dynasty
39 Chang'an Lu. Tel. (029) 5261633
唐乐宫　长安路 39 号
Located south of the Bell Tower, opposite the Xi'an Hotel, the complex boasts a world
class theatre restaurant with extensive banqueting facilities and an authentic Cantonese
restaurant. The theatre restaurant can comfortably seat 500 diners and is the only one of
its kind in China. Whilst enjoying a menu which blends the best of East and West, diners
are serenaded by musicians playing authentic Chinese classical instruments. Dinner is
followed by an hour-long cultural show of traditional music, song and dance replicating
the entertainment of the Tang dynasty court (see also page 38).

Baiyunzhang Jiaozi Restaurant
Bell and Drum Tower Square. Tel. 7214636
白云章饺子馆 钟鼓楼广场
A Muslim restaurant which serves Hui-style *jiaozi* (dumplings). Their speciality, a set of *jiaozi* (six different kinds including mutton, mushroom, seafood) is recommended.

Defachang Jiaozi Restaurant
Bell and Drum Tower Square. Tel. 7214060
得发长饺子馆 钟鼓楼广场
Located next to the Bell Tower on the square, this newly renovated restaurant was originally established in 1936. Beijing-style dumplings here are as attractive as the restaurant's name, 'Flourishing Virtues'. Many kinds of *jiaozi* are tasty and served in a visually appealing way, such as 'Two Dragons playing with a Pearl' and 'All Flowers Exposed to the Sun'.

Tongshengxiang Paomo House
Bell and Drum Tower Square. Tel. 7217512
同盛祥饭庄 钟鼓楼广场
A *paomo* and mutton hotpot banquet at this unpretentious restaurant is excellent value and is one of the most authentically chinese experiences in town. Another of the renovated restaurants adjacent to the Bell and Drum Tower Square, on the edge of the Muslim quarter, and well patronized by locals. The banquet menu includes varied *hors d'oeuvres* and traditional *paomo* (dry starchy bread broken into small pieces and submerged in hot, lightly spiced mutton broth), but the most recommended dish is a Mongolian-style hotpot cooked at the table. You hold thinly sliced raw meat with chopsticks in the boiling water of the hotpot to cook for a few seconds, then flavour it with a variety of sauces. This is followed by 'dragon's moustache' soup, madewith long rice noodles and vegetables.

May the First Restaurant (Wuyi Fandian)
351 Dong Dajie. Tel. 7120804
五一饭店 东大街 351 号
This downtown restaurant alongside the Foreign Language Bookstore is popular for banquets and provides local-style food. There are two snack restaurants on the first floor serving, among other things, Chinese snack food such as *baozi* (steam dumplings) and *wonton*.

Xi'an Restaurant (Heping Branch)
88 Heping Lu. Tel. 7437895
西安饭庄分店 和平路 88 号
This is the former Peace Restaurant, now serving Shaanxi-style dishes and local snack banquets. Its menu still includes Peace Restaurant specialities such as *chao babao* and *qinxiang shaomai*.

Xi'an Restaurant (Xi'an Fanzhuang)
298 Dong Dajie. Tel. 7216120
西安饭庄 东大街 298 号
The largest restaurant in the city occupies a huge six-floor block with containing 14 dining rooms. There is little discernible ambience. Food is officially Shaanxi style, and many of the delicacies, such as *kaoyangrou* and *yangrou shuijiao*, are available; however, the chefs are flexible and can cook other kinds of Chinese cuisine. The calligraphy of the sign in front of the building is by Guo Moruo, a literary eminence of the People's Republic.

Qingyazhai Restaurant
384 Dong Dajie. Tel. 7281881
清雅斋饭庄 东大街 384 号
This is also a Muslim restaurant run entirely by Hui, or chinese Muslims. They specialize in lamb and vegetable dishes. Especially good are lamb *jiaozi*.

New China Snacks
Dong Dajie.
新中华 东大街
Between the Dong Dajie Department Store and the Qingyazhai Restaurant (see above), on the south side of the road, is a small but typical sweet snack shop. Everything is very cheap and the best way to order is to point. Fried glutinous rice, covered with sugar and containing red beans, is one favourite. Another is sweet congee, rice porridge in syrup with peanuts or *baihe*, lily bulb.

Muslim Food Street
Damai Shijie.
大麦市街
This street in the west of the city, off Xi Dajie, comes alive in the evening and is certainly worth a visit—if only to stroll, soak up the atmosphere and observe the array of snacks and food on offer and watch them being prepared, if you don't have the courage to actually try anything.

Useful Addresses

Regent Holidays
15 John Street, Bristol, BS1 2HR, England. Tel. (0117) 9211711; fax 9254866;
e-mail: 106041.1470@compuserve.com; http://www.regentholidays.co.uk

Abercrombie & Kent (Hong Kong) Ltd.
19/F Gitic Centre, 28 Queen's Road East, Wanchai, Hong Kong. Tel. (852) 2865-7818;
fax. (852) 2866-0556; e-mail: pmacleod@abercrombiekent.com.hk

TRAVEL SERVICES IN XI'AN
China International Travel Service, Xi'an Branch (see page 15 for more details)
48 Chang'an Lu. Tel. 5262066
中国国际旅行社西安分社 长安路 48 号

China Travel Service, Shaanxi
Xingqing Lu. Tel. 3244352
陕西省中国旅行社 兴庆路

China Youth Travel Service, Shaanxi
90 Hongying Lu. Tel. 5256415
中国青年旅行社陕西分社 红缨路 90 号

Overseas Travel Corporation, Shaanxi
32 Chang'an Beilu. Tel. 5261516
陕西海外旅游总公司 长安北路 32 号

TRANSPORTATION
China Northwest Airlines Booking Office
296 Xishaomen (outside west gate). Tel. 8702193
中国西北民航售票处 西稍门 296 号

Dragonair Booking Office
Lobby Floor, Sheraton Xi'an Hotel, 12 Fenghao Lu. Tel. 4262988; fax. 4203097
港龙航空公司 西安喜来登酒店 丰镐路 12 号

SHOPS

Wenbaozhai Store
5 Yanta Lu. Tel. 5532380
文宝斋旅游购物中心 雁塔路中段 5 号

Xi'an Special Arts & Crafts Factory
138 Huancheng Xilu. Tel. 8623128
西安市特种工艺美术厂 环城西路北段 138 号

Foreign Languages Bookstore
349 Dong Dajie. Tel. 7212197
陕西省外文书店 东大街 349 号

MISCELLANEOUS

Bank of China, Shaanxi Branch
233 Jiefang Lu.
中国银行陕西分行 解放路 233 号

Bank of China, Xi'an Branch
52 Honghui Xiang, Tanshi Jie.
中国银行西安分行 炭市街红会巷 52 号

Long-distance Telecommunication Office
Xixin Jie.
西安长途电讯局 西新街

Post Office
1 Bei Dajie.
西安市邮政局 北大街 1 号

Shaanxi Province Travel Bureau, Office for Tourist Complaints
15 Chang'an Beilu. Tel. 5261437 (Mandarin and English)
陕西省旅游局旅游举办公室 长安北路 15 号

Foreign Affairs Office, People's Government of Shaanxi Province
272 Jiefang Lu.
陕西省人民政府外事办公室 解放路 272 号

Shaanxi Provincial Hospital
19 Youyi Xi Lu. Tel. 5251331
陕西省医院 友谊西路 19 号

Fourth Army Medical University Hospital
Changle Lu. Tel. 3374114
第四军医大学医院 长乐路

**Division of Aliens and Entry-Exit Administration of the Xi'an Municipal Public
Security Bureau**
138 Xi Dajie. Tel. 7275934
西安市公安局出入境管理处 西大街 138 号

Index